Extraordinary Leaders 卓抜の指導者

World War II Memoirs of an American Naval Officer and an
Imperial Japanese Naval Officer

AuthorHouse™
1663 Liberty Drive
Bloomington, IN 47403
www.authorhouse.com
Phone: 1 (800) 839-8640

Published by AuthorHouse 10/02/2015

ISBN: 978-1-5049-5007-7 (sc)
ISBN: 978-1-5049-5008-4 (hc)
ISBN: 978-1-5049-5019-0 (e)

Library of Congress Control Number: 2015915512

Print information available on the last page.

This book is printed on acid-free paper.

Extraordinary Leaders 卓抜の指導者

World War II Memoirs of an American Naval Officer and an
Imperial Japanese Naval Officer

Joseph E. Jannotta, Jr.

Jay and Sue: good friends and count you both for support; thanks.

Joe Jannotta

authorHOUSE®

To Gina and Yoshiko,
and their grandchildren

CONTENTS

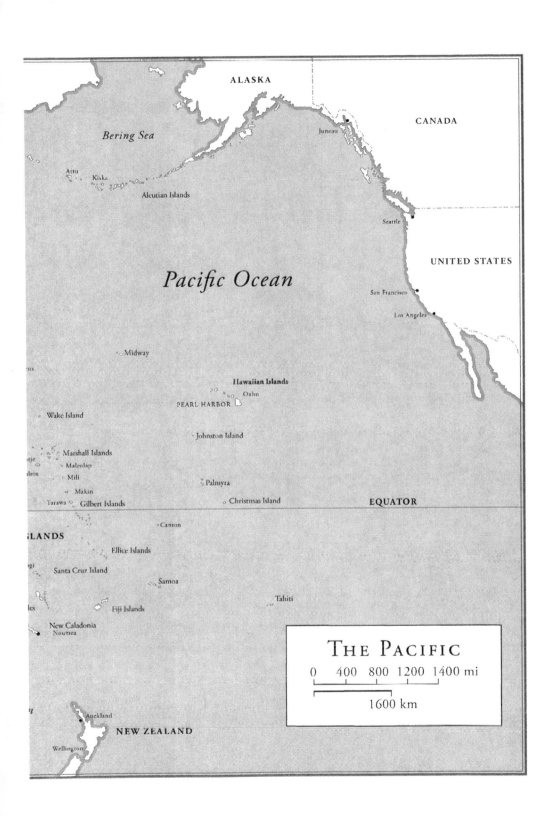

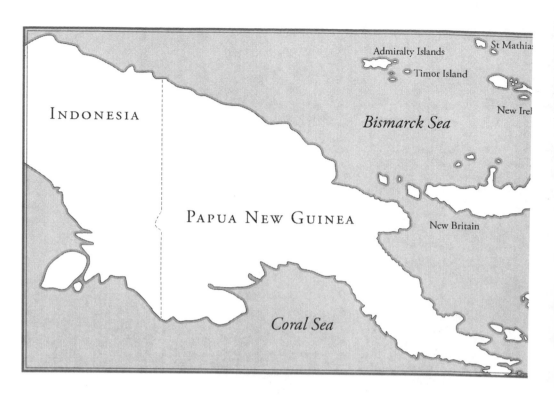

SOLOMON ISLANDS AND VICINITY

Mathias Group

Tabar Islands

Lihir Islands

New Ireland

Tanga Islands

Rabaul

Feni Islands

Green Islands

Pacific Ocean

0   50   100   150   200 mi

200 km

Solomon Sea

Buka Island

Bougainville Island

SOLOMAN ISLANDS

Choiseul Island

Shortland Island
Treasury Islands

Santa Isabel

Vella Lavella Island

The Slot

Trobriand Islands

New Georgia Island
Rendova Island

Malaita

Woodlark

Russell Islands

Florida Islands

D'Entrecasteaux Islands

Guadalcanal

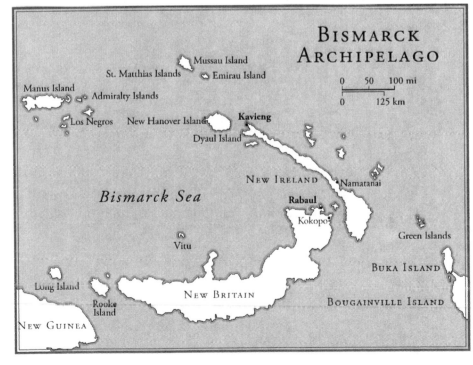

BISMARCK ARCHIPELAGO

Mussau Island

St. Matthias Islands

Emirau Island

0   50   100 mi

0   125 km

Manus Island

Admiralty Islands

Los Negros

New Hanover Island

Kavieng

Dyaul Island

NEW IRELAND

Namatanai

Bismarck Sea

Rabaul

Kokopo

Green Islands

Vitu

BUKA ISLAND

Long Island

BOUGAINVILLE ISLAND

Rooke
Island

NEW BRITAIN

NEW GUINEA

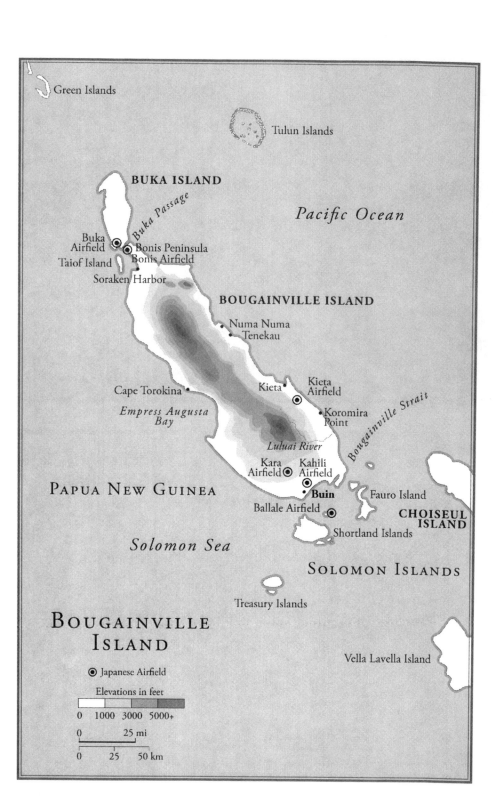

Green Islands

Tulun Islands

BUKA ISLAND

Buka Passage

Pacific Ocean

Buka
Airfield
Bonis Peninsula
Bonis Airfield
Taiof Island
Soraken Harbor

BOUGAINVILLE ISLAND

Numa Numa
Tenekau

Cape Torokina
Kieta
Kieta
Airfield

*Empress Augusta
Bay*
Koromira
Point

Bougainville Strait

Luluai River

Kara
Airfield
Kahili
Airfield

PAPUA NEW GUINEA

Buin
Fauro Island

Ballale Airfield
**CHOISEUL
ISLAND**

Shortland Islands

Solomon Sea
SOLOMON ISLANDS

BOUGAINVILLE
ISLAND

Treasury Islands

Vella Lavella Island

◉ Japanese Airfield

Elevations in feet

0   1000 3000 5000+

0   25 mi

0   25   50 km

Lives of great men all remind us
We can make our lives sublime,
And, departing, leave behind
footprints on the sands of time.

HENRY WADSWORTH LONGFELLOW

Lieutenant Joseph E. Jannotta USNR, Rear Admiral A. Vernon Jannotta USNR and Edgar Dalzell Jannotta USNR. Photo taken at the Admiral's 50th wedding anniversary in New York City, 1968.

Why this Book?

One January night in 1953 I sat at the officers' club bar at the US Naval Base in Norfolk, Virginia, where men drank and told stories to pass a chilly evening. I could only worry about my own predicament. A newly commissioned carrier pilot, I'd received my orders earlier that day and my mind had been tumbling ever since—I was headed to Korea.

I was uncertain about the importance of this United Nations "police action" and not at all sure how to feel about the prospect of getting shot at in a war that didn't seem to matter in the big picture.

I picked up the phone and called my father's oldest brother, Vernon Jannotta, then a captain in the Naval Reserve and a veteran of both World Wars. I could picture my uncle, a proud man with blue eyes and a big Roman nose. In the winter of 1950-51, I had lived with him in his Evanston, Illinois home. I thought of him as he looked when he was striding around his study, carrying his 5' 6" frame as if he were 6' 6" tall, telling me stories of fighting in the Pacific.

In those stories, Uncle Vernon conveyed a palpable sense of certainty in what he and his men had been fighting and, in some cases, dying for. As I nursed my beer, I heard my uncle's stories again in my head, and I wondered if I would have the same sense of purpose about fighting in Korea. Unlike World War II, the political imperatives of this war seemed less obvious. As I was connected to his New Jersey home, I was vaguely aware that my intentions were to ask if he could pull strings and get me duty anywhere other than Korea. It seemed plausible. My father's brother was up for promotion to rear admiral and was well known and respected among the Navy brass.

After a brief hello to Aunt May, Vernon's voice came through with its usual graveled rasp. I told him my news.

"Isn't that the worst luck?" I said.

"Are you kidding? That's great news, Joe. Congratulations," my uncle said. Without missing a beat, he went on about how wonderful it was that I'd get to put my training to use in wartime service to our country. "Nothing could be more important."

I hung up the phone, not feeling much better, despite my uncle's clarity on the matter.

In the end, I spent an intense period flying carrier missions over Korea until an armistice was declared July 16, 1953, a truce still in effect today. I came to believe that my uncle had been precisely right in congratulating me. He was speaking from the same core belief that had led him to rejoin the Navy during World War II at age 47—the necessity of serving one's country in time of war. Back home from combat, time and distance improved my vision. Korea was not just a "police action," but also an important moment for the United States in the Cold War.

Fortuitously, years later, Uncle Vernon's grandson, Henry Vernon Nickel, sent me Uncle Vernon's WWII letters to his wife—I say fortuitously since I had sold my business and here was an undertaking of special interest. As a Navy lieutenant commander, Uncle Vernon had commanded 12 148' amphibious infantry landing ships called Landing Craft Infantry Large, or LCI Ls, in the Solomon Islands, and subsequently as a commander, he skippered 48 LCI Ls in the Philippines. In these campaigns he earned a Navy Cross, a Silver Star, two Bronze Stars and a Purple Heart. As I read the letters, I was struck by his direct presence at some of the Pacific War's most important battles. I speculated: wouldn't it be fascinating to compare Jannotta to an Imperial Japanese Naval officer who fought and wrote about the same naval battles as Jannotta, to see the war from two different perspectives? That began a quest to find the appropriate Imperial Japanese Naval officer.

Initially I met with Rear Admiral David Polatty, USN, Commanding Officer of Great Lakes Naval Bases. He and I had represented the US Navy in the reopening and dedication of Chicago's Midway International Airport, named after the Navy's Pacific War victory off Midway Island in June 1942. We became friends. Over dinner one night, I shared with him Uncle Vernon's Pacific War writings and the idea of finding an Imperial Japanese Naval officer who fought and wrote about many of the same battles as Jannotta. Might there be an opportunity to compare their combat experiences? Admiral Polatty was enthusiastic about the concept and, following an e-mail correspondence with him in which I outlined my thoughts for a juxtaposed combat writing of an American and a Japanese officer, introduced me to Japanese Vice Admiral Toshio Muranaka. I made a trip to Japan and spent a day with Admiral Muranaka and his colleague Captain Shinten Kukita. They carefully, yet graciously, discussed my background and my ideas that would compare a Japanese naval officer's combat diary to Jannotta's letters to his wife. In the end they introduced me to the Fujimoto family. The deceased father, known during the war as Lieutenant Kotarō Kawanishi (he took his wife's family name in a 1948 marriage), had published a book, *Records of Wars on Bougainville Island by an Imperial Japanese (Navy) Officer*. It contained diary entries of his combat experiences in the Solomon Islands and, like Jannotta's letters, they were well written, giving the other side of the story. I speculated: might not the letters and diaries of these two men contain the substance of a book?

To start, their accounts provide an immediacy to the Pacific War, etchings that illustrate in-the-trenches (and from-the-sea) views. Rather than the more typical top-down study, this is a bottoms-up approach to looking at the War.

In reading Jannotta's and Kawanishi's experiences, the issue of leadership surfaces. I came to the project carrying stereotype notions about Japanese military leadership, rating it top down and directive in style, or even at times physically brutal in dealing with its men. I was in for a surprise, both in terms of style and quality of leadership, when I read of Kawanishi's experiences. "A sample of one," you say? There had to have been other Japanese leaders sitting in Japan's hierarchical and structured society who exhibited Kawanishi's basic human decency amidst all of the violence.

Since the subject of leadership is an underpinning theme of this book, one might ask what my qualifications are to address it.

My professional career began as a corporate human resource officer at Jewel Companies, Inc. of Chicago recruiting, identifying and developing talent for senior levels. In 1976 I resigned from Jewel and founded a national career counseling firm, Jannotta, Bray and Associates, a company that assisted terminated senior executives transition to new work. As chairman, I played a central role in the management of the firm for 18 years until its sale to Right Management, Inc., a NASDAQ stock exchange company. My last relevant experience, in 2007 and 2008, was to serve the Secretary of Defense on a seven-member advisory committee at monthly meetings studying and recommending changes to military compensation.

Also, at the behest of Secretary of Defense Donald Rumsfeld, I was asked to counsel, *pro bono*, members of his staff (Generals, Admirals and Assistant Secretaries) who were transitioning to civilian positions. Rumsfeld wanted to make sure each one made a successful transition to civilian life. He cared about them and that caring extended to his troops in the field and to the wounded where he made regular Sunday visits to the hospital. I witnessed the Secretary's genuine human commitment to his men.

My professional work assignments typically required substantial assessment work with the client, with key elements being a three-hour biographical interview by a senior consultant such as myself, a half day with a psychologist, and two hours' of feedback by the consultant and psychologist discussing the client's profile and potential next positions. Often the assessment work included "360-degree" interviews of the client's bosses, peers and subordinates, a confidential procedure done with terminating company's and client's approval; it's a process pioneered by our company.

To assist in my assessment work, our firm used a form to make leadership judgments. It included a statement on family factors as well as the following traits related to decision-making abilities, organization and management, leadership, courage, communications, pressure, and interpersonal skills, including environmental factors that underpin personal success.

A skill that didn't get much attention were interpersonal capabilities. Both Jannotta and Kawanishi excelled at these skills. They exhibited a concern for the well-being of their men, a human element central to their leadership. Kawanishi found himself in a difficult moment between Japanese soldiers and the Buka natives at a time of rape and murder. Kawanishi offered a plan that enabled the survival of most of his men and the natives.

In editing the writings of these two men during a war that is now more than 70 years behind us, the anger, prejudice and preconceptions can be stripped away. The two men come into sharp focus. Their stories become universal and provide lessons of life for our grandchildren.

Alfred Vernon Jannotta, 1917.

Chapter I

EARLY YEARS OF JANNOTTA

The entire man is, so to speak, to be seen in the cradle of the child.

ALEXIS DE TOCQUEVILLE

It was Ensign Jannotta's sixth round trip transporting US troops to France when his ship, the cruiser USS *San Diego*, struck a German mine off the US East Coast and sank. After five hectic hours in the 55-degree Atlantic they were picked up by a Dutch freighter and off-loaded the next morning into an empty Hoboken, New Jersey warehouse where they faced a new problem. The crew had lost everything—money, personal effects and clothes, except for the salt-crusted uniforms they were wearing. Uncle Vernon telephoned his mother's brother in Short Hills, New Jersey, and borrowed $2,000 so that he could loan each of his men $10.

Over the next several years some of the money dribbled in, repaid by the sailors. The last payment came eight years later in the summer of 1939. Jannotta, then the CEO of Tapp, Inc., a high-end manufacturer of bedroom furniture, was riding up a New York City building elevator on his way to a customer meeting. Absorbed in reviewing his plans for the sales call, he suddenly became aware of a man in his thirties staring at him.

"Aren't you Vernon Jannotta?"

"Yes, I am."

The young man reached into his pocket and pulled out a $10 bill.

"I served under you on the USS *San Diego*. Sorry to be so late, but here's the money I owe you."

Later sitting in a Manhattan bar drinking a scotch, the encounter with his shipmate triggered waves of memories: his leap from the sinking USS *San Diego's* rising keel into the ice cold Atlantic, giving his life jacket to the sailor who couldn't swim and the intense fear he felt when he thought he might be sucked under by the sinking ship.

Back in his suburban Chicago home Vernon told his wife, May, of his New York City encounter with his shipmate. Hoping to find his Navy records that might include the sailor's name and address, he began a search. With May's help—she was an interior decorator and the attic was her territory, full of samples and materials—they rummaged through it until they found a dusty, wooden footlocker with his name painted on top: "LTJG Vernon Jannotta, USNR". Included in it were his Oak Park High School and Cornell University records as well as his Navy files, but no record of the sailor's name. Of note, though, were his high school grades: he achieved an "A" average during his four years at Oak Park High with the exception of one "C" (which the high school registrar told me on a phone call, might have been due to an illness). Truth known, his academic achievements were in part due to the watchful and ambitious eye of his mother, Stella Skiff Jannotta, on her first son. Her aspirations included Vernon running the family-founded, -owned and -operated Jewel Tea Company. His mother, a liberal activist, was also dead set against smoking tobacco and drinking alcohol. She suspected Vernon was a user, and in a letter written at the time of his high school graduation she admonished him that grades weren't enough. "Do not forget that you will do no good if you do not lead a clean life. There is only one way. Self control. Then you can look the world in the eye. Make me a proud mother, Vernon."

The record shows despite her admonition, Uncle Vernon entered Cornell University, threw clean living to the wind and dove into Cornell University social life. He joined a fraternity, sang in the Glee Club, formed and played in a dance band, took weekend trips to New York City, and mostly partied. His academic record suffered and by his senior year, he was on probation.

But what interested Uncle Vernon most was the war in Europe. He asked his mother's permission to join the Ambulance Corps in France. On April 2, 1917, before she could respond, President Wilson declared war on the German/Austrian Axis. This time Vernon didn't wait for permission. He enlisted in the Navy with his entire Cornell class. When Stella found out on April 9, 1917, she wrote to him,

Stella Skiff Jannotta

"It breaks my heart that you have already enlisted." An avowed pacifist, her high expectations for her first son didn't include military service.

Regardless, Vernon was committed, and it wouldn't be long before that commitment would be tested. In May 1917, Seaman Recruit Jannotta reported to the US Naval Academy at Annapolis, Maryland, for basic training, and enthusiastically embraced Navy life. By mid-July he was promoted to Chief Petty Officer. Then, following five days of competitive exams and two screening interviews, he received notification that he was to be commissioned an Ensign in the US Navy Reserves. In a September 8, 1917 letter to his mother, a youthful Jannotta shared the news:

> Oh, I was never so happy in my life. To be recommended for commission immediately was great enough, but to know

the Commandant and his staff considered me to be good enough to send out to duty with the fleet...is the realization of my ambitions and hopes of the last six months—and it's more than that, because it is more than I had hoped for.

Here's another glad surprise I received the other day. Of course all this time I had charge of Company D—a mighty fun bunch of men, too—drilling them and whipping them into shape. Well, last Saturday they were all shipped out—sent across. Just before they left, I had called them to attention and was going to tell them how sorry I was I wasn't going with them, when one of the men stepped out of the ranks and handed me a package as a token of "esteem," he said from Co. D. I opened it up, and it was a small watch, with the engraving on the back: "Presented to A.V. Jannotta, C.Q.M., by Co. D, September 1, 1917." Well you could have knocked me over with a feather I was so surprised. That was pretty darn nice of them, wasn't it?

When I receive my appointment, I've promised a bunch of my friends here a dinner party and blowout. Can I ask you for the money or not, Mother? If not, just say so, and I can put them off.

Give my love to all the folks. Can't you and Margaret (adopted sister) come and visit me here next week? Please try, Mother. You know I get awfully homesick.

Loads of love,
Vernon

Uncle Vernon was assigned to the USS *San Diego*, a cruiser that convoyed US troops to Europe. On his sixth trip, near Long Island, when the *San Diego* struck a mine, Jannotta was standing watch high up in the mainmast. In the intense excitement of the moment, he thought he saw a submarine—"something straight, slender and dark"—and directed the port broadside guns to fire.

At this point, the *San Diego* developed a serious list and the increased angle made the guns inoperable. A cease-fire was ordered.

For the first time, with the intense excitement of the past few minutes, Jannotta became conscious of his surroundings. His mind shifted from firing guns to the condition of his ship.

He recorded the event in a memoir written September 1931:

We were no longer moving. The starboard engines were now dead, too. And we were settling by the stern and heeling over fast; a good 18-degree list at least. The water had reached the port quarterdeck, and as I looked down from on high, I seemed almost to be hanging over the sea. I saw no one but a small group of sailors stationed at the depth bombs on the quarterdeck, hanging onto the chute and the rail to keep from sliding down the deck into the water.— God, she was certainly going over! I could almost see her roll. Looked at the water creeping up the deck on the low side! —Heard a crash? Something big broke over the port side then—That turret was going to slide in soon!—How long before the mast snapped? It couldn't lean clear over the water like this much longer.

I looked at the men with me. Men? No, just youngsters like me. Tense, questioning—but not afraid. Good boys, these. Yet no sound, since the last futile, ear-splitting crash of the guns. Everything was so still. The sea, the ship, the wind, all seemed hushed. Slowly, surely—but quietly, so strangely quietly—the *San D* was going over. Why didn't the skipper say the word? Be too late in another minute. Then—the clear, high notes of a bugle, from up forward on the bridge. It sounded "ABANDON SHIP"—once, twice, three times.

To my sailors on the voice tubes, "Gun crews abandon ship." Now to the two men with me, "Over you go, don't try the port side—take it to starboard." We scrambled one after the other over the side of the control-station rail—and down the mast.

Already, hundreds were swarming over the starboard side of the ship. Men were sliding, jumping, dropping into the water. Life rafts, mess tables, Kapok mattresses, preservers—anything that might float and was nearest to hand—were being hauled or hurled overboard too, for a man-of-war carries no lifeboats. Sick and injured were all being carefully lowered in hastily made slings, and men, swimming, towed them to nearby rafts. Cool and collected officers directed as division after division, section after section, group after group of sailors went over the side. Not a second to lose—but no panic here. A splendid, almost unconscious discipline.

I reached the foot of the mainmast and glanced quickly around. Looked like most everyone was off. I couldn't stand upright on the boat deck now, the list was so great. I scrambled to the starboard edge of the boat deck—slid down its side—then a jump, and I pulled myself up to the rail of the main deck. Over I climbed. Out to starboard were hundreds of men swimming, struggling, in the water. The deck was almost at right angles to the water. Two others, an officer and a sailor, were climbing to the rail with me. "Got to hurry," one said, half aloud.

I slid—the others with me—over the curving side and bottom of the ship as she rolled—to the bilge keel as it came up from the water—and then, as the keel was quickly rising, a wide-flung leap to the sea, five or six feet below. As I struggled to the surface, only one thought—to get away from her before she made her final plunge. Get away as far as possible. Her boilers might explode—the ammunition—the depth bombs! My God, the depth bombs. The safety pins were pulled when we went into action. They'd blow us all to hell and gone. Swim and kick as I would, I could not seem to get away from the ship. A suction kept pulling me back, alongside of her. Was I going to drown after all? For a moment I panicked. For the first time in all those crowded minutes preceding, I felt the ice of fear contract my heart. Thoughts of home, of mother, sweetheart, flashed through my mind. I didn't want to die.

Then I realized my frantic strokes were taking me away from the ship. My mind cleared. I became calm, and swam more coolly, for perhaps a hundred yards. I forgot myself, and thought of the ship, the *San D*; turned round, and treaded water. She was full bottom up now. Slowly, ever so slowly, she was sliding down, stern first, into the water. Men forgot for the moment their own predicament and watched her final moments. The forward end rose higher, higher. When a half of her length was under, she paused, quivered. Then, with a rush and rumble of water, she disappeared below the surface of the sea. Choppy swells, foamy water, bubbles, to mark the spot. The *San D* was gone.

I glanced at my watch. It had stopped—1122—the moment I had struck the water. It couldn't have been twenty-three minutes after that time that she'd gone down. That would make it eleven twenty five. God, that was quick work. Hit at 1105—gone at 1125. Only twenty minutes! It had seemed like hours—so much had happened.

As the torpedoed USS *San Diego* plunged from view, Ensign A. Vernon Jannotta became alert to a chaotic seascape—heads and debris bobbed everywhere, mingled with cries of shipmates finding their buddies.

Within minutes, conversations dropped to a minimum; the focus became survival in 55 to 60 degree Atlantic waters. To maintain circulation, Jannotta kept both legs and arms moving. Others were having more serious difficulties. Someone cried, "Help!" Jannotta located a sailor with no flotation aid and with the help of two other men, Jannotta removed his life jacket and put it on the sailor.

The sinking of the *San Diego* was Uncle Vernon's closest encounter with combat and death during World War I. He served out the remainder of his enlistment without serious incident, and after the war returned to Cornell to finish his bachelor degree; then he entered the business world.

Kotarō Kawanishi at graduation from the
Naval Accounting School.

Chapter II
EARLY YEARS OF KAWANISHI

Like Vernon Jannotta, Kotarō Kawanishi's adult achievements were shaped and foreshadowed by his family upbringing and his society's culture.

A fundamental premise underlying American anthropologist Ruth Benedict's research is that human behavior—be it of a Buka tribe or an entire nation—"is *learned* in daily living." Her landmark study of the Japanese during WWII, *The Chrysanthemum and the Sword*, pondered a simple question: why were Japanese troops willing to fight until death, rather than surrender? It represented a paradox that, for her, begged systematic research. So Benedict set about studying the "deeply entrenched attitudes of thought and behavior" learned in the daily social experience of Japanese and, in her words, find "what makes Japan a nation of Japanese."

Both the US and Japan looked at each other using their own cultural lens, seeing and judging the other through their respective beliefs and doctrines. Equality-driven Americans, for example, viewed the Japanese strict adherence to hierarchy (in which each individual takes his prescribed place in society) as illogical or, worse, irrational. Conversely, the Japanese saw winning the war as "the victory of spirit over matter." It amounted to pitting American faith in 'things' against Japanese faith in a 'spirit' that was handed down over more than a thousand years by the divine and legendary Emperor Jimmu. For a Westerner, it's not an easy cultural tenet to grasp.

Benedict illustrates this disconnect with a Japanese wartime radio broadcast about an air force captain returning from a combat mission. The Japanese captain landed, dismounted from his plane and, gazing through binoculars, accounted for his squadron. He then proceeded to headquarters and made his report to the commanding officer, at the end of which he collapsed.

> *The officers on the spot rushed to give assistance but alas! He was dead. On examining his body it was found that it was already cold, and he had a bullet wound in his chest, which had proved fatal. It was impossible for the body of a newly dead person to be cold. Nevertheless the body of the dead captain was cold as ice. The captain must have been dead long before, and it was his spirit that made the report. Such a miraculous fact must have been achieved by the strict sense of responsibility that the dead captain possessed.*

To an American, this tale seems bizarre, but not to Japanese of that time. If a thousand-year-old spirit can be transmitted to the emperor's descendants, why can't the discipline or spirit of a dead captain last two hours?

—◦◦◦—

Much of what we know of Kawanishi's childhood depends largely on his unpublished autobiography, which was generously made available to me by his son, Takahiro Fujimoto. Written late in his life, the writing recounts his family history and describes his childhood up to the age of 12.

Kotarō Kawanishi was born to Shokichi and Hide Kawanishi, who brought their first-born son into the world on April 26, 1919, in a downtown Tokyo ward. At their house in one of the world's fastest-growing cities, Shokichi and Hide would produce a family of five children in eight years—an eldest daughter, then Kotarō, two more daughters, and another son. With Hide's daughter from a previous marriage—she had buried two husbands before meeting Shokichi—

there were eight in the Kawanishi family.

Raising a small child and widowed twice before, Hide's third marriage was something of an unlikely match. She had been born into the prosperous Kofu brewing family and, despite her somewhat ordinary appearance, often had suitors. Her first marriage had ended in tragedy. Shortly after she gave birth to a son, her husband died. The dead man's family sent Hide back to her own family, but they kept the son so he could follow in the father's business. She became a "cold-rice relative," a cast-off woman without standing in her in-laws' family and without claim to her own child.

Broken-hearted, she took a job as a seamstress at a large department store. She remarried, gave birth to a daughter, and once again her spouse passed away. With a daughter, there was no fuss over custody. Widowed for a second time, and again with a young child, she met a handsome illustrator, Shokichi Kawanishi, who courted and married her.

Shokichi Kawanishi had moved to Tokyo from the city of Ikeda, on the outskirts of Osaka. He prospered as an artist, marketing his skill as a calligrapher. He strode through the avenues of Tokyo with good looks and a style tailored to the Western fashion that prevailed in Japan's urban centers during the early 20th century. Years later, his son marveled that this man, who was so fond of a good party, would have ended up married to Hide. "He was a handsome man: medium-build, good physique, and vaguely reminiscent of (Clark) Gable. He was what in common terms would be called a pleasure quarter aficionado. Being a tasteful, attractive man, he was widely popular in the red light district."

His son Kotarō Kawanishi's earliest memory at age four was the Great Kanto Earthquake on September 1, 1923. He documented his recollections in his autobiography:

In an open air space there is a pile of gravel. We stand there petrified, all the siblings with our mother. The sky in front of us is red, on fire. This is the scene. At the time we lived on 26 Hamamachi Ayamegawa-kishi on the bank of the Sumida River.

11

When the earthquake hit, my father promptly hired a boat and loaded all our household items and us children, and tried to escape via the river. All around was a sea of flames and with four children on board he was not able to go very far. As the fires spread it became impossible to be in the river. The ashes from the fire flew through the air and set some boats ablaze. Down the river came a burning boat. Rushing ahead full tilt, Dad strove to turn as to avoid a collision, while at the same time wiping off the ashes from our boat and sprinkling water on our belongings. There came other larger boats and Dad transferred Mom and us onto one of them while he stayed on the smaller boat trying to put out the fire. At this point the wind blew the two boats apart and Dad stayed on the smaller boat and drifted away. At sunset the next day we got off the boat onto the burning ruins on the bank. Mom seemed absent minded, she was with four of her children but her husband was missing. An unfortunate circumstance.

Fortunately, two days later my father and his apprentice returned home safely. It was an emotional moment.

Kawanishi carried these memories with him the rest of his life. The event set the stage for the terrible fire bombings in Tokyo, March 9 and 10, 1945.

Despite Shokichi Kawanishi's financial success, the family began to suffer. Though Japanese culture tended to segregate concerns of the wife from a husband's social pleasures, Shokichi's womanizing exceeded the approved norm. Eventually, he squandered his reputation. By the time her son was six, Hide had had enough, deciding to separate herself and the children from their father. She moved the family out to Setagaya, one of many rural villages that lay just beyond the industrial mass of Tokyo, claiming it was better for the children's health. It was a bold, highly liberated move for a Japanese wife to make, but Shokichi went along with the arrangement, partly because it left him alone in the city where he was free to do as he pleased.

It was an abrupt change. Kotarō noted his new school, "a forlorn, puny, dull wooden building in the fields," shocked him. And the students magnified his feelings. "They were all small, dark, and dressed in Japanese robes. Nobody wore *hakama* (traditional men's trousers that included a formal kimono); not a single person wore Western style-clothes. Everybody wore dirty, splashed-pattern Japanese robes." Even their rural dialect sounded unrecognizable. He felt like a foreigner.

While his classmates eyed him suspiciously, their teacher introduced him:

> *This is Kotaro Kawanishi. From now on, he will be studying with us. He comes from a school in Tokyo. He is a very proficient student, so everyone must work hard to keep up with him. Please, be friends with him.*

During lunch break, everyone assembled around Kotarō, asking him questions he didn't understand. In his journal he wrote:

> *One of them said, "Let's wrestle!" His buddies moved the desks to make room. The classroom turned into a wrestling ring. Malnourished but tall and strong, I won the first three rounds. Someone came to the rescue.*

Kotarō went on to defeat two more opponents—victories that gave him immediate status with his classmates.

In third grade, Kawanishi got a new teacher, Miss Omata.

> *She had a close-cropped head and wore the close-buttoned student uniform. But she was young, enthusiastic and lively. She applied the old rules and punishments—hitting us on the head and making us stand—but she was bright and openhearted, and the students loved her. As head of my class I had numerous occasions to be in contact with her; I was hit on the head more often, and treated with affection more often. She would call my name, "Koo-ta-rooo," and*

ask me to take care of various errands, at times unrelated to school. I was annoyed.

Miss Omata became Kawanishi's teacher and mentor until his graduation from elementary school. At his mother's urging, he planned to attend a prefecture-run middle school; however, only 15 students were admitted to that school each year, and no one from Kawanishi's school had ever earned admittance. In his fifth year, and as preparation for the exam, Miss Omata began assigning Kotarō extra work that included going to her house in the evenings for additional assignments. She was on a mission, recalled Kawanishi:

(She) would assign me a problem and then go take a bath or do other work while I solved it. I'd call her once I finished and if I did not understand she hit me on top of my head. As a result, I did my best to figure the problem out.

I have one or two memories from the days when I went to Miss Omata's house. At about the same time, a number of immigrants from Tokyo joined our class— although they looked more like sixth-year students. Among them there was an adorable girl, Nakamura Yoshiko. She was my first love, I think. At my age, this was the kind of thing one kept to oneself. I did, and treated her coldly, although it was uneasy and unbearable. She was such a gentle girl, like nothing I had ever seen in school before.

One day, as always, I was at the teacher's house to do extra work. Miss Omata brought out the quizzes she had given us in class that day, and asked me to check them and mark the mistakes. This would be unthinkable nowadays, but it used to be quite common. She went to take a bath. There I was, alone, grading everyone's tests. I came to Yoshiko's. It was maybe a 60—a terrible score. I wondered, "What can I do?" I could not simply change the score; I had to change the entire test. I had no idea how to do it. This was a crime. I would betray the teacher's trust. It was serious. Yet I could not bear the thought of giving Yoshiko a 60. I was surprised at how much pain can build up in a small heart. I erased parts of the exam and rewrote them, made it an 80-point test, and quickly put it back in the stack. My heart beat furiously. I thought, "What if Miss Omata walks in and discovers me?" It felt like the end of the world. I had committed my first crime. The following day, as the teacher gave back the exams, I breathed a sigh of relief. At the same time, the spell broke, and all my feelings for Yoshiko disappeared. When one is a child, the sense of shame is so strong that even affection succumbs to it.

In the Japanese home, children are typically taught to respect themselves, which refers to living up to others' expectations. The fear of shame and the resulting ridicule and loss of face are powerful sanctions in their culture.

In the end, Miss Omata's mentoring succeeded. Kawanishi passed the prefecture middle school exam and entered it at age 11; it set him on a course to enroll in a first rate university and ultimately to receiving an Imperial Japanese Naval commission.

At home, his mother dedicated herself to the well being of her children, "and I was the core of her dedication. It was as if we still lived in the medieval period: I, as the eldest son and family heir, received a preferential treatment over my brother and sisters. In return, I was supposed to uphold the family name and make it strong against its enemies, as I was told time and time again. My brothers and sisters may have not liked it, but whenever we were in that certain mood, the 'family head' mentality sprung up in all of us."

Leadership, responsibility and authority became habits of Kawanishi from a very early age. Like other Japanese youth, he learned his place in the family and carried those lessons into society as a military officer and businessman. By taking one's proper place in society—a centuries' old hierarchy sequenced by Emperors and noblemen, samurai warriors, farmers, merchants, and laborers—social order and security were maintained on this island chain that crowded 70 million people.

Kotarō remembered one scorching hot summer when he and his mother went to her uncle's house in the town of Ise.

It must have felt like her real home. It was a huge building, with a large garden that opened up by the tall veranda, showing all the grace and splendor of an old family. Being a child I thought, "This is unbelievable! It is impossible to build a house like this!"

It seemed like mom had attached all her dreams onto me, and I was annoyed by all the words of encouragement and moral lessons.

Despite his occasional frustration with his mother's preaching, her expectations provided him with a life-sustaining motivation that drove his achievements. Other personal traits that bolstered his accomplishments were superior intellect, a dominant physical presence, a soft or feminine side, and an independence of action.

Kawanishi's upbringing in Tokyo and Setagaya largely coincided with the maturation of Japan as a modern, global power. It began in July of 1853 when Commodore Matthew C. Perry steamed four US Navy battle ships into Edo Bay, present-day Tokyo, and demanded Japan open its borders to trade. Ultimately, Commodore Perry's actions triggered the crisis that brought down the Tokugawa Shogunate; the overthrow culminated in 1868 when rebels proclaimed the restoration of imperial rule under Emperor Meiji. Out of the revolution emerged a gifted group of young samurai (Meiji oligarchs) who feared that Japan, like China, might become a puppet of the Western powers.

The oligarchs determined to use Western tools to prevent Western incursions. They set Japan on a course of modernization and industrialization that reshaped the nation into the mold of Western democracies.

Two events—the Great Depression and the Manchurian Incident of 1931—were the catalysts that ultimately brought conservative forces to power. The Manchurian episode involved a group of zealous Japanese army officers who, acting on their own, bombed the Southern Manchurian Railway tracks near Mukden, China, and blamed the local Chinese warlord for not keeping the peace. Using it as a pretense, Japanese army forces began a series of military maneuvers that resulted in the occupation of the three provincial capitals of Manchuria. By 1933, the Imperial Japanese Army occupied all of Manchuria; a puppet government was installed and Manchuria renamed Manchukuo.

As world opinion turned against Japan's military aggressions, an aroused League of Nations voted overwhelmingly to censure Japan. To further exacerbate Japan's political crisis, junior army and navy officers attempted two coups, in 1932 and 1936. While both of them failed, the cowed politicians took the nation further right. One consequence was an increasingly muzzled press.

When Japanese troops advanced into Beijing in 1936, relations with the US, already difficult, worsened. President Franklin Roosevelt regarded the aggression as a violation of China's right to political self-determination. And as accounts of terrible atrocities in Nanjing and other cities reached the US (news that never was reported to the Japanese public), American attitudes hardened. On the other hand, the Japanese saw themselves as liberating Asians from Western colonialism and they resented America and Europe's anti-Japanese sentiments, sentiments that only served to fuel the country's nationalism.

As the Japanese military continued to extend control to Shanghai, Canton, Hankow, and the Hainan Islands, the US imposed economic sanctions as a way of pressuring the government to moderate its policies. The failure of US policy became apparent when Japan occupied southern French Indochina in July 1941. President Roosevelt answered by freezing all Japanese assets in the US. Despite last-ditch negotiations between Washington, DC and Tokyo, hard lines were already drawn and war all but declared, a war that would draw millions of young Japanese into it, including the young university graduate, Kotarō Kawanishi.

Naval Accounting School, Section 4, Unit 22. Kawanishi is in the front row, second from right.

Japanese attack Pearl Harbor the morning of December 7, 1941. *US Navy*

Chapter III
SUNDAY, DECEMBER 7, 1941

On Sunday afternoon, December 7, 1941, Vernon Jannotta sat in the library of his suburban Kenilworth, Illinois, home reading the *Chicago Daily Tribune*. As an avid follower of the events in Europe and the Pacific, Jannotta must have found the day's news troubling:

FDR SENDS NOTE TO MIKADO AS JAPS MOVE TOWARD THAILAND. Washington, DC, Dec. 6 President Roosevelt addressed a personal message to Emperor Hirohito of Japan, as the State Department received word two heavily escorted Japanese convoys were steaming from French Indochina into the Gulf of Siam (Thailand).

The article went on to speculate that the President's message to the Emperor might have included a personal plea for peace. It also reported that 18,000 Japanese troops had boarded 21 transports in Camranh Bay and French Indochina, a move that might foreshadow an attack on Thailand, aimed at cutting the Burma road which supplied China.

The news from Europe was equally negative. The headline read:

MOSCOW FACES DIREST PERIL, LONDON HEARS

It reported that 1,500,000 Axis troops threatened to overrun Moscow and other Soviet cities. "How much worse can things get before we're at war?" reflected Jannotta. With that he pushed the *Tribune* aside, pulled his stamp collection off the library shelf, and began to paste recently purchased stamps into one of several catalogs. As a Chicago Bears football fan he then tuned in the Bears and Chicago Cardinals game on his Philco radio. Both the game and his stamps provided Jannotta welcome moments of ease. The president and owner of Tapp, Inc. a Chicago furniture manufacturer, he worked a six-day week. His schedule included meetings with customers and suppliers, sales conferences, visits to his plant to pour over manufacturing schedules and, of course, to control expenses. Tapp had only recently begun to break even, so Jannotta and his controller monitored the company's cash position daily. His coming week would be no different—or so he thought.

Suddenly, the radio announcer broke in:

"We interrupt this broadcast to give you a news flash: the Imperial Japanese Navy has attacked the US Navy and Army installations at Pearl Harbor, an attack that began at 0700 Hawaiian time. I repeat, the Imperial Japanese Navy bombed Pearl Harbor early this morning in a surprise air force strike. The extent of the damage, as of yet, is unknown. As more details become available this station will inform you."

"Good Lord!" Jannotta exclaimed, jumping to his feet, "This means war." To his wife he shouted, "May, come quickly. You must hear this."

The next morning, the *Chicago Tribune's* lead article summarized what he had been hearing on the radio:

RAIDERS BLAST HONOLULU, ARMY AND NAVY BASE HIT—US BATTLESHIP SUNK IN FIGHT A Japanese aircraft carrier succeeded in getting close enough to the Hawaiian Islands to launch wave after wave of dive-bombers, unmolested by Navy patrols. According to a Tokyo dispatch, these bombers sank

the United States battleship *West Virginia* and
several destroyers and set the battleship *Oklahoma*
afire in Pearl Harbor. It was stated further that 300
American military airplanes were destroyed on an
airfield by Japanese bombers.

That morning, Jannotta and Tapp's staff gathered in the
conference room to hear President Roosevelt ask Congress for a
declaration of war. It was a somber scene repeated all over America:
in homes, on streets, in drug stores, plants, military installations,
and schools where student bodies assembled to hear the President's
declarations.

Shortly after 1000 Central Time President Roosevelt began his
famous "date of infamy" speech:

"Yesterday, December 7, 1941—a date which will live in infamy—the
United States of America was suddenly and deliberately attacked by
naval and air forces of the Empire of Japan."

The President went on to say the attack had caused severe damage
to "American naval and military forces...very many American lives
have been lost." He followed with more bad news: Japanese attacks
had hit Malaya, Hong Kong, Guam, the Philippine Islands, Wake
Island, and Midway Island.

"Hostilities exist. There is no blinking at the fact that our people, our
territory, and our interests are in grave danger. With confidence in our
armed forces, with the unbounding determination of our people, we
will gain the inevitable triumph—so help us God."

Uncle Vernon was deeply moved. As a WWI veteran and a
determined patriot he again offered his services to the Navy and
subsequently sent a telegram to the Navy Department with his offer.

Author's note: From this point on the manuscript is written as a historical document
as opposed to a personal memoir, thus the terms "Jannotta," "Lieutenant Commander Jannotta," and "Commander Jannotta," replace the personal salutation,
"Uncle Vernon".

In the middle of the Pacific Ocean, the international dateline divides each calendar day along an imaginary boundary placed at 180 degrees longitude. Thus the day Americans will forever know as Pearl Harbor Day was, in Tokyo, December 8, 1941. On the following day, the 9th, outside Hitotsubashi University, Kotarō Kawanishi gathered with several fellow students at a sidewalk café to hear what they anticipated would be an important announcement. For just such momentous occasions, the Japanese government had installed a nationwide system of loud speakers on the streets of its towns and cities. Kawanishi was within six months of completing his undergraduate degree at Hitotsubashi, one of Japan's top universities. He planned to join the Toshiba Corporation after graduating but also faced a commitment to the Imperial Navy's Supply and Finance Corps. If things worked out, he would first join Toshiba as a management trainee and later report to active navy duty as an ensign.

At the duly appointed hour, the speakers crackled to life and the citizens of Japan learned the news of the Pearl Harbor raid and the stunning Japanese victory. In the Hitotsubashi area, the reaction was immediate. The crowds erupted. Kawanishi and his classmates clapped and cheered and joined the street celebrations. In his speech, General Hideki Tōjō, the Japanese Prime Minister, talked about "annihilating" America and its allies, all of whom he accused of trying to dominate the world. At the end of the broadcast, a favorite patriotic song, *Umi Yukaba*, blared forth:

> *Across the sea, corpses in the waters;*
> *Across the mountain, corpses in the field,*
> *I shall only die for the Emperor,*
> *I shall never look back.*

A year later, the Japanese and Americans had fought furious battles at Coral Sea and Midway, and were currently fighting at Guadalcanal. Now 22, Kawanishi was training to be a supply officer in the Japanese Imperial Navy. He had finished his university courses, earning a degree in business administration, and briefly worked with Toshiba Corporation before being inducted into the navy in September 1942. His orders sent him to supply corps paymaster school in Tsukiji. There, training began at 0600 and ended at 2200 each day except Sunday. The young navy inductees sat through eight hours of classes followed by three additional hours of demanding physical exercise—rowing, swimming, soccer, basketball, baseball, and *sumo* and *judo* wrestling. In sumo and judo, Kawanishi distinguished himself, placing first and second respectively in his class of 450.

The question of whether to remain in the homeland or to serve on the front lines of the Pacific War had been easily answered by most of the men in Kawanishi's class of paymasters: they chose the factory. So did Kawanishi. In January, at the end of his four-month training period, Kawanishi requested duty as weapons inspector at a factory in Tokyo.

This result outraged Kawanishi's chief instructor, Lieutenant Junior Grade Kozama. "Why did you join the navy at all?" he demanded. "Everybody is applying for homeland assignments and nobody wants to fight as a military man." Kozama's indignant outburst rattled Kawanishi.

With this thundering voice, we were asked to resubmit our assignment requests.

I wanted to live comfortably no less than any other man, but Kozama's voice had its effect on me. My superiors had earlier told me that transfers were frequent in the navy and that it would be better anyhow to be assigned to a difficult place first, because you would then be transferred into an easier place after a year or so. So then and there I resubmitted my request saying "request to work at the front in the south." This decided my fate.

※※※

It took more than nine months for Vernon Jannotta to re-enter the Navy. Since no immediate buyer for Tapp Furniture could be found, the business had to be placed in the hands of the minority shareholders. By September, with his personal affairs in order, Jannotta, at age 47, took his Navy physical. In preparation, he spent six months running on the Lake Michigan beach that fronted his Kenilworth home and passed with flying colors. The only negative was his false teeth, a fact the Navy chose to ignore. On October 6, 1942, he was sworn in as a Lieutenant Commander, United States Navy Reserve, and received his orders to report to Norfolk, Virginia, Amphibious Force Atlantic.

On Thursday, October 15, 1942, Jannotta described the train ride from Chicago to Norfolk in the first of many letters to his wife, May. "The train was absolutely crowded—95% in the military service." He met a sailor who had been at Pearl Harbor at the time of the attack and another sailor who had been on the aircraft carrier *Lexington* when it was sunk at the Battle of Coral Sea. Their stories helped Jannotta adjust to military life. "I wish everyone in the country could have ridden that train with me. It was an awakening and an inspiration to me at any rate," he wrote.

While riding the ferry to Norfolk, he observed an aircraft carrier, a cruiser, transports, destroyers, and supply ships, all without names, only numbers. Mistakenly, the cab driver took him to the headquarters of Admiral H. Kent Hewitt, Commander Atlantic Amphibious Force at a converted seaside summer resort where he spent the night instead of the Amphibious Operations headquarters at Norfolk. Senior brass were everywhere. They talked about "a big, audacious, powerful force" being formed that could only mean one thing, Jannotta wrote to his wife: a major invasion.

In fact, Jannotta was witnessing the final stages of preparations for the US landings on the northwest African coast in an operation named Torch. It was a first step in the "Hitler first" Allied strategy. As commanded by Rear Admiral Hewitt, the US would make three separate landings of 35,000 troops under Major General George S. Patton on November 8, 1942: Casablanca, Port Lyautey and Safi in the northwest corner of Africa. Two other landings by the British with

American support were also planned near Oran and Algiers, Algeria. They were initial steps to ultimately recapturing French Morocco, Algeria and Tunisia from Germany and Italy. It amounted to a compromise strategy for General George C. Marshall, US Chief of Staff who argued for landings on the French coast in Europe; however, Prime Minister Churchill and the British Joint Chiefs were dead set against it, pointing out that the Allies were neither trained nor equipped for such an undertaking. "D-Day" landings on the French coast would wait until June 1944.

In the Pacific, the early days of 1942 were dark and foreboding for the United States, an apparent invincible Japanese military defeated the Allies in the Philippines, Hong Kong, Malaya, Singapore, and Java. Three battles in the spring, summer and fall of 1942 altered that outlook: The Battles of Coral Sea, Midway, and Guadalcanal. Before reviewing these battles, a look at America's and Japan's leadership and their strategy for winning the war.

Historian John Caldwell in his book, *Strategic Architecture*, points out the importance of war expert, Carl Von Clausewitz's cardinal caveat:

"The first, the supreme, the most far-reaching act of judgment which a statesman and commander have to make is to establish— the kind of war on which they are embarking—This is the first of all strategic questions and the most comprehensive.

Roosevelt understood this and aligned the political, military, and commercial forces of America "in an existential fight to the finish where the loser would have to face total defeat." His leadership changed every sector of American life and converted him to a transformational leader (versus a transactional leader).

In contrast, Fleet Admiral Isoroku Yamamoto and Japan's military had a different strategic view: Japan had never lost a war, their victories were quickly achieved. The Russo-Japan War is a case in point, on May 27-28, 1905, when the Japanese fleet under Admiral Heihachiro Togo decisively crushed the Russian fleet at Battle of Tsushima; it effectively terminated the war. Japan's Pearl Harbor attack had a similar aim: a total victory that would bring America to the bargaining table—and finesse the ramp-up of the US industrial might. Yet three issues made the attack less successful—one, the offensive arm of the US Pacific Navy, its three aircraft carriers were not in port and escaped destruction requiring a follow-up effort at the Battle of Midway. Second, the "surprise attack" on Pearl Harbor deeply angered Americans and rather than seek peace, stood solidly behind their president in search of a total military victory. Finally, Japan's delay initiating actions following their Pearl Harbor victory gave Admiral Ernest J. King operational breathing space to make key personnel changes that began with the appointment of Admiral Chester W. Nimitz to commander in chief of the Pacific Fleet on December 31, 1941, who in turn began to make his own personnel changes.

Back to the three game changing battles.

BATTLE OF THE CORAL SEA
May 3-8, 1942

On May 3, 1942, a Japanese invasion force under Vice Admiral Takaki made up of 14 transports, 2 heavy and 1 light aircraft carrier, 8 cruisers, and 12 destroyers sailed out of their Rabaul Naval Base, marking the beginning of the Battle of Coral Sea. Japan was pursuing a two-staged operation: invade the Solomon Island of Tulagi to establish a naval base, and follow up by landing troops at Port Moresby, New Guinea, some 200 miles from Australia. Both were possible precursors to isolating Australia from the United States.

Admiral Chester Nimitz ordered Rear Admiral Jack J. Fletcher, based on code-breaking intelligence, to put his task force—aircraft carriers *Yorktown* and *Lexington*, 8 cruisers, and 11 destroyers—into the path of the larger Japanese force, hoping to surprise it. But what occurred were a series of exploratory maneuvers by each side to locate its enemy. On May 7, the task force found and sank the Japanese light aircraft carrier *Shoto*, while Japanese pilots sank the US destroyer *Sims* and the oiler *Neosho*.

The next day, the Japanese aircraft carriers *Zuikaku* and *Shokaku* and the United States carriers *Yorktown* and *Lexington* faced off. At times only 100 miles of sea separated the two forces. In the mêlée, all four aircraft carriers were hit by torpedoes and dive bombers, with the

Lexington incurring a fatal explosion below deck from leaking aviation gas. Both sides broke off the action at the end of the day on May 8. As US Navy historian Samuel E. Morison points out, the Battle of the Coral Sea was the first carrier-against-carrier sea battle in naval history. It resulted in a tactical victory for the Japanese in terms of ships sunk, but due to the US sinking of the carrier *Shoto* the invasion of Port Moresby was called off. It proved to be a strategic victory for the United States.

BATTLE OF MIDWAY
June 4-6, 1942

During the Battle of the Coral Sea, Japanese military leaders were in the midst of plans to invade Midway Island. The Japanese Commander, Admiral Yamamoto, devised a complicated strategy: send a small fleet consisting of two aircraft carriers, two heavy cruisers, and

US Navy Douglas SBD-3 "Dauntless" dive-bombers from the aircraft carrier *USS* Hornet, June 6, 1942. *US Navy*

an occupational force north to invade the Aleutian Islands and draw American Naval forces away from Midway; then using four separate elements of the Imperial Japanese Navy—submarines, a task force with four attack aircraft carriers, an occupation force, and a main body of battleships, cruisers and a light aircraft carrier—invade Midway. This mass put at Yamamoto's command the largest war fleet ever assembled in modern times. By all logic, the battle should have resulted in not only the capture of Midway Island, but also the destruction of the United States Navy's Pacific Fleet. Yet the success of the operation, observed Morison, depended on surprise and an expected enemy behavior.

However, the US Navy proved uncooperative. At Pearl Harbor, a combat intelligence group made up of 100 men under Lieutenant Commander Joseph J. Rochefort, an officer with an amazing recall of intelligence details, broke the Japanese naval code and learned of the pending attack. Admiral Chester Nimitz, Commander of the Pacific Fleet, acted on the information and directed his task force commanders to place their ships on the flank of the enemy fleet. On June 4, when American patrol planes located the Japanese Fleet, Rear Admirals Raymond A. Spruance and Frank J. Fletcher timed the launch of planes from the aircraft carriers *Enterprise*, *Hornet* and *Yorktown* hoping to catch Admiral Yamamoto's four carriers at a particularly vulnerable moment—in the act of rearming and refueling recently returned aircraft from an initial Midway Island strike. When the first American aircraft arrived over the Japanese task force they were slow-moving, low-flying torpedo bombers that were systematically destroyed by anti-aircraft fire and Zero fighters (Japanese long-range fighter aircraft). But the action placed the Zeros at deck level, so that when the US Navy's Scout Bomber Douglas (SBD) dive bombers arrived over the enemy at 14,000 feet, they were unopposed. The SBD had dive brakes which when deployed, enabled the pilots to make their dives at an 70% angle, thereby increasing the accuracy of their bombing runs. As the US Navy pilots rolled into their dives they looked down on carrier decks lined with bomb-laden, fully gassed aircraft all about to be launched against the American fleet. Timing in life is everything. Had the SBDs arrived 45 minutes later, following the launch of the Japanese air fleet, the Battle of Midway would have had a different outcome.

As it turned out, the US Navy dive-bombing runs turned Japanese carriers *Kaga, Hiryu*, and *Soryu* into fireballs, and seriously damaged the *Akagi*, which was later scuttled. On June 7, an impaired and listing *Yorktown* took two torpedo hits from the Japanese submarine I-168 and sank. Regardless, Midway was a staggering US victory. On June 8, in addition to four Japanese aircraft carriers and a cruiser, the Battle of Midway claimed 250 Japanese aircraft and close to 100 trained and experienced aviators—a blow from which the Imperial Japanese Navy never recovered.

BATTLE OF GUADALCANAL
August 1942 to January 1943

The Midway Victory offered the chance for a major strategic initiative by the US and its Allies. Admiral Ernest J. King, Chief of Naval Operations didn't disappoint, in a history-making dispatch on June 25, he proposed that the US Navy undertake landing on the Solomon Island of Guadalcanal. It was a close call, given that the Japanese had a

US Marines wading through shallow water, Guadalcanal, Solomon Islands, August, 1942. *US Army*

military edge on the sea and in the air—plus the fact that the European theater supposedly had priority over the Pacific in allocation of men and materials. Nevertheless, President Roosevelt approved the plan. On August 8, 1942, the Navy landed 19,500 marines on Guadalcanal as well as three neighboring Solomon Islands. The initial landings succeeded, but the Japanese counter-attacked. The battle began slowly and picked up in intensity, both sides sensing that the winner would be on the offensive from that point on.

In the period of August 1942 to January 1943, seven major sea battles were fought: the Battle of Savo Island (August 8-9), Eastern Solomons (August 24-25), Cape Esperance (October 11-12), Santa Cruz (October 26), two battles of Guadalcanal (November 12-13 and November 14-15), and Tassafaronga (November 30). The first battle, Savo Island, a night engagement, resulted in a stunning Japanese victory over a less experienced and prepared US fleet. It triggered Admiral Chester Nimitz, Commander in Chief of the Pacific Fleet to critically analyze the fleet's readiness, especially its night operations and in the process Admiral Nimitz placed major emphasis on training (practice, practice).* These sea battles produced a tonnage loss of 126,420 for the US and 134,839 for the Japanese fleets close to equivalent. However, the Japanese losses were irreplaceable given their industrial base (see chart on page 39 illustrating the dominance of America's ship building capabilities over Japan's.)

The land Battle for Guadalcanal between the US Marines and the Japanese troops produced constant air combat and jungle warfare. Both sides built up their ground forces. The Japanese committed 36,000 men and the US 60,000. In the end, the US prevailed, but it took six months. The victory enabled the US to take the offensive in the Solomon Islands as demonstrated by the US Navy's amphibious forces.

During the month of October, when the Battle for Guadalcanal was at its most ferocious and its outcome in doubt, Jannotta waited for his assignment to amphibious forces. His turn would come.

---

*As a naval aviator, friends ask me how was it possible to do the seeming impossible, to land on an aircraft carrier under way? My response is training. When the time comes you're ready. Therein lies one of the US Navy's secrets to success.

United States President Franklin D. Roosevelt and
British Prime Minister Winston Churchill with their advisors in Casablanca,
Morocco, 1943. Standing second from left: Admiral Ernest J. King.

Chapter IV
STRATEGIC OVERVIEW

As 1942 came to a close, Allied victories in French North Africa, Coral Sea, Midway, and Guadalcanal raised the question, "Where to from here?" To answer it, President Roosevelt, Prime Minister Churchill and their military staffs planned to meet at Casablanca in January 1943. In anticipation of the meeting, Admiral Ernest J. King, Commander in Chief of the US Navy Fleet prepared a strategy for the Pacific War that would create a defining role in bringing America's industrial might to bear.

Initially, he met with Admiral Chester Nimitz, Commander in Chief of the Pacific Fleet in San Francisco. Nimitz proposed moving up the Solomon Islands from Guadalcanal with landings in the middle Solomons to establish air bases there. It would be an important step in neutralizing a series of Japanese air bases, five in the Solomons and five surrounding Rabaul, New Britain. Until this was accomplished, no offensive could be directed to the critical objective of recapturing the Philippine Islands. Furthermore, the victories at Midway and Guadalcanal were achieved by the slimmest of margins. The US couldn't afford to overreach now and any new initiative would require a substantial increase in manpower, ships and planes. King fully supported Nimitz's recommendations.

From the war's onset, the US and Great Britain had been committed to a "beat Hitler first" strategy, and it was a starting point for any Allied planning. Notwithstanding, Admiral King made a rough estimate in mid-December 1942 of where American dollars were allocated in the war effort. He found that only 15% of the monies were deployed to the Pacific Theater. The rest went to Africa and Europe. King, with the support of General George C. Marshall, Chief of Staff, reasoned that the momentum achieved against Japan might be lost unless sufficient men, ships and planes were set aside for the Pacific. Furthermore, since the Allies would not be prepared to launch Operation Overlord (the cross-channel invasion of France) until 1944, King argued that an adjustment in favor of commitments to the Pacific Theater was in both America's and Britain's best interest.

The British, however, were strongly opposed to a reallocation of resources. With this dynamic at play, the British began to take King's measure. Following the first day of the Casablanca conference on January 14, 1943, Sir Ian Jacob, secretary to the British Chiefs of Staff, made these notes in his diary, "King is well over 60 but active, tall and spare with an alert and self-confident bearing. He seems to wear a protective covering of horn, which is hard to penetrate. He gives the impression of being exceedingly narrow-minded and to always be on the lookout for slights and attempts to put something over on him. His manners are good as a rule but he is angular, stiff, and finds it difficult, if not impossible, to really unbend. I am convinced, however, there is much more to him than appears on the surface." In general, his British Royal Navy counterparts felt he resented "American resources being used for any other purpose than to destroy Japan."

Throughout the conference King was unyielding, a position implicitly backed by a president who tended to give his senior military staff more latitude than the hands-on Churchill. King's stance was bolstered by the fact that he controlled the deployment of landing ships and craft without which there could be no European offensive. As a consequence, the British agreed to a bargain. It amounted to a doubling of Allied men and materials earmarked for the Pacific. In return, the US would support the British-preferred "Mediterranean Strategy" of invading Sicily and Italy.

JAPAN'S STRATEGIC POSITION VIS-À-VIS US

Japan's Fleet Admiral Yamamoto well understood America's industrial power, having studied at Harvard University, worked at

Japan's Washington, DC, Embassy and traveled the US in the late 1930s. "If I'm told to fight (the US) regardless of the consequence, I shall run wild for the first six months or a year, but I have utterly no confidence for the second and third years," Yamamoto is quoted as saying in "Memoirs of Prince Fumimaro Konoye".

In 1943, with its broad strategies for Europe and the Pacific now in place, America ramped up its industrial might to a staggering degree. Nowhere was it more obvious than in the construction of aircraft carriers, the primary offensive weapon in the Pacific War. Seven CV aircraft carriers were commissioned by the US Navy in 1943, including *Essex* (CV-9), launched on December 31, 1942. In addition, 9 Light and 48 escort aircraft carriers were built for the US Navy. In the construction of destroyers (DDs) and destroyer escorts (DDEs), America's mass-production capability played a dominant role: 125 DDs and 222 DDEs rolled off assembly lines in 1943. To support the fleet's offensive operations of aircraft carriers, battleships, cruisers, destroyers, and submarines, the US built thousands of oil tankers, minecraft, cargo ships, tugs, repair tenders, hospital ships, torpedo boats, and landing ships and craft including 1,089 LCIs, the ship Jannotta commanded. In manpower, the contrasts between the two powers were also significant. On December 31, 1941, US Naval officers and enlisted men on active duty totaled 383,150. A year later, the number had risen to 1,259,167. By the end of 1943, US Navy manpower totaled 2,381,116. In contrast, the increase in Imperial Japanese Navy officers and enlisted men was anemic: from 311,359 at the end of 1941 to 429,368 in 1942. The importance of America's industrial might in the Pacific War is captured in the graph on page 39, comparing Japan's manufacturing capabilities to build battleships, carriers, cruisers, destroyers, and submarines to that of the US.

This astounding capacity is what inspired Prime Minister Churchill to exclaim, when the United States entered the war in late 1941, that "England would live—Silly people, and there are many, who might discount the force of the United States" as soft. As a student of the Civil War, with all its intensity, sacrifice, and bloodshed, Churchill knew better. He recalled a remark made to him 30 years earlier by Sir Edward Grey who likened the US to "a gigantic boiler.

Once the fire is lighted under it there is no limit to the power it can generate."

Regardless, Jannotta and Kawanishi would soon see the effects of the US's manufacturing strength with their own eyes as well as its importance in the defeat of Japan. It explains Japan's drive to destroy the US Navy's fleet with quick blows at Pearl Harbor and later in the Battle of Midway with a small, well-trained and elite fleet. It is worth noting in Evans and Peattie's book "Kaigun" that Japan's Imperial Navy personnel losses at the lieutenant commander and commander levels were impossible to replace due to its defeats at the Battle of Midway and the Solomon Island campaigns.

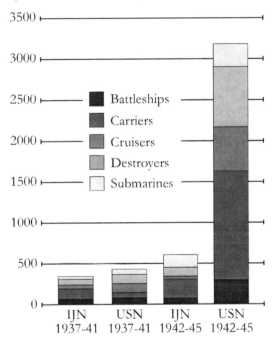

Standard Tons Displacement
(Number in Thousands)

Imperial Japanese Navy (IJN) and US Navy (USN) shipbuilding, major
combatants built, 1937-41 and during World War II. Based on data in
David Evans and Mark Peattie, *Kaigun: Strategy, Tactics, and Technology in the
Imperial Japanese Navy, 1887-1941*, fig. 10-2, page 467.

Admiral Isoroku Yamamoto saluting pilots at Rabaul about to embark on
"I-Go" operation, April 11, 1943. *US Navy*

Chapter V
ADMIRAL YAMAMOTO'S DEATH

In February 1943, Ensign Kawanishi disembarked from the cruiser *Suzuya* at Rabaul, headquarters for the 8th Fleet, and began an assignment in supply and finance. His work was not glamorous, nor, at first, dangerous. It entailed supplying materials to Japanese Solomon Island bases at Bougainville, Kolombangara, New Georgia, and Rendova.

However, his health became a problem. "I got sick," wrote Kawanishi, "and suffered from a kind of fever within less than a month since I had started my new post in Rabaul. Although I had been told that it was a kind of disease everybody got there, I suffered terribly from it." Kawanishi recovered, but a month later was hospitalized again, this time with typhoid.

Kawanishi remained in the hospital for more than a month. "At that time," he wrote, "the Japanese Army was pushing and there weren't many air raids by the enemy. On one day, Admiral Isoroku Yamamoto visited the patients in the 8th hospital where I was. He was directing the Combined Fleet from his headquarters at Rabaul. I sat up on the bed and saluted him. He noticed and returned the salute with a grand expression. He was a pillar of the navy and a person on whom the whole nation depended. I was deeply moved."

By May 1943, Kawanishi returned to headquarters and found the atmosphere depressing, though he wasn't sure why. There had been recent staff changes which he decided might be a source of the problem, or perhaps it was because the main power of the combined fleet had moved to Truk. But then he learned some highly confidential news from a staff member, his friend Ohashi—Admiral Yamamoto had been killed when his aircraft was shot down in mid-April near Buin, Bougainville.

I couldn't believe that Admiral Yamamoto died within two weeks after he had visited me in the 8th hospital.

"Ohashi, you are lying, aren't you?"

"Yes, it is true, the whole senior staff is shocked," said Ohashi.

When I came to realize this as fact, I felt like I had been hit on the head with an iron hammer. "When was it?" I asked.

"A while back, probably the 18th."

Only a few days a after he visited me in the hospital.

This was not good. The first thought that ran through my head was, "It's all over. We are going to lose the war." We had a kind of faith in Admiral Yamamoto; a belief that things will go well as long as he was with us. But the Admiral was dead.

The atmosphere at the headquarters was very depressing. Nobody talked aloud. Everybody was very quiet. No one drank alcohol. Everybody left the table as soon as they finished their meals. Everybody was shocked and not able to talk about his death. Because of a "gag mandate" it wasn't until later that the Admiral's death was formally announced.

The air raids by the enemy became increasingly more frequent, changing the atmosphere in Rabaul. The state of the war, which wasn't going well, did not allow us time to mourn the Admiral's death.

In July, Kawanishi received orders to report immediately to 8th Fleet Naval Base at Buin, Bougainville. He expected the transfer would put him in the middle of "real fighting." The shock of Admiral Yamamoto's death and the withdrawal of the Combined Fleet "had me prepared for the worst" and since Bougainville would be the enemy's next assault target, the transfer seemed like a "suicidal leap into the abyss."

On July 10, he packed and prepared to depart:

Leaving a trail of dust and exhaust, the plane circled the Vulcan Crater volcano (Simpson Harbor, a caldera) and headed toward Buin. Looking down, I saw that most of Rabaul had been transformed into a burned-out wreck, a sight vastly different from the one I saw when I first arrived.

We flew over New Britain and soon came to the sea and headed south. Glittering blue ocean spread out as far as the eye could see. It wasn't long before Bougainville came into view, a large lush green island—completely covered in green vegetation—floating in the azure sea. Emerald green lagoons surrounded the coastline. The only feature that wasn't green was the yellowish banks of the rivers that sliced across the island. From the air, this South Pacific island was a sight of fantastic beauty. How could such a place be a battlefield?

Already, the plane was approaching Moila Point. By air, the trip from Rabaul to Bougainville was quite short. The problem was traveling between the two places over water. This is the place where Admiral Yamamoto died. As I recalled the event and reflected on the shock I felt when I learned of Admiral Yamamoto's death, the plane's PA abruptly announced that a squadron of enemy planes was attacking Buin airfield, our destination.

The bomber lowered its altitude and circled the area. We flew in the shadow of the mountains, hiding in wait until the air raid ended. If an enemy plane spotted us, we would be helpless against it. For 40 tense minutes we waited. Finally, a communication came in saying that the attack had ended and the enemy squadron had withdrawn. Greatly relieved, our tension subsided. Our plane approached the airfield. Landing the plane on a runway pock marked with craters from daily air raids— not to mention the attack just 10 minutes earlier— was no easy task. After making several passes, the pilot decided on a landing path. The plane touched down and shook violently from side to side. Finally, it came to a stop. I would remember this as the first of many ordeals that I somehow managed to survive.

We got out of the plane and ran all out for the air raid bunker in the jungle on the edge of the burning airfield. If enemy aircraft caught us out on open ground, we were finished. The air force officers watched us in bewilderment, wondering what had gotten us so worked up. For these men, an attack by a squadron of enemy planes was just another part of the day. I felt quite foolish. They didn't even bother to evacuate the control tower on the side of the runway during the attack. I had come up through the ranks as a staff officer, and I again reminded myself that I was about to become a part of the real fighting.

Kawanishi's assignment required planning the supplies for Bougainville. But the Allied offensive against neighboring islands Munda, Rendova and Kolombangara had left Japanese forces there desperately short of supplies. So Kawanishi had to figure out how to sneak supplies to those men. Most of the resupply missions required the use of destroyers brought from Rabaul to ferry supplies under cover of darkness. "Keeping one's nerve and wits was a challenge," penned Kawanishi.

Our ground units feverishly prepared for the next enemy landing; and within this tense, siege-like atmosphere I saw the best and worst of men. Claiming to be suffering from bad nerves, the Chief Paymaster for the First Landing Group took to his quarters and wouldn't come out under any circumstances. This infuriated staff officers who berated and beat him to get him to come out. But the man passively resisted every effort to rouse him to action, and they finally gave up and replaced him—which required a precious plane to fly him back to Japan.

This Chief Paymaster was in fact our superior and mentor and his egregiously unsoldierly behavior deeply chagrined us. But we all get though life in our own way.

Allied air raids typically targeted airfields, but one day the bombing strategy shifted—to Kawanishi's headquarters and living area. Bombs began to fall and caught everyone by surprise. Kawanishi knew he was in mortal danger when a bomb exploded in front of his barracks. He dove into the air raid shelter.

That was the first near miss. The roar and shaking from the explosion made me think my head had been split in two. For a while I couldn't move. All around me, men collapsed onto the ground, one on top of another. Some babbled incoherently, others cried. The shelter lay half in ruins. Dirt and dust from the debris tumbled inside and blinded me. I finally regained my composure, and putting on a brave front said, "We're safe now." Only a pillar remained standing of the barracks I was in but a moment ago. I gazed at the bizarre sight of my raincoat, with maybe a third of the lower portion torn away, hanging from the pillar obliviously flapping in the ocean breeze. The palm trees were stripped bare of their leaves, their scorched trunks exposed to the blazing sun.

Kawanishi's narrow escape was one of many signals of the Allies' increasing dominance. Few places offered any real shelter to Japanese soldiers anymore.

USS *LCI L 335*, USS *LCI L 328* and USS *LCI L 336* landing US troops and supplies at Rendova in the Solomon Islands, July 4, 1943. *US Navy*

Chapter VI
LANDING CRAFT INFANTRY LARGE
(LCI L), TRAINING AND COMBAT

Jannotta's entire Pacific War experience entailed commanding the newly designed Landing Craft Infantry Large, initially as a commanding officer (CO) of a group of 12 and later as a flotilla CO of 48 LCI Ls.

These innovative, purpose-built ships played an essential role in the Pacific Theater where ocean expanses had to be crossed fully loaded. But LCI Ls were less appropriate at Normandy, which required a short channel crossing that beached 1,000,000 men in one action.

On October 21, 1942 at the Amphibious Training Base in Maryland, Jannotta met and interviewed with Commander Chester L. Walton, the designated Commanding Officer of a new flotilla of 48 LCI Ls.

As a result of the meeting, Commander Walton selected him as the first CO to command a group of 12 LCIs. Jannotta was thrilled. A week later, he reported to Galveston, Texas, where he and Commander Walton took delivery of their first two LCIs. Looking at the LCI, Jannotta judged they would play an essential role in landings across the Pacific. "But for now," he noted, "only two things were clear: almost no one had any experience aboard these newly invented ships, and they would have to learn fast, because the LCIs were built for (future scheduled) combat assaults."

Jannotta described Commander Walton as "a real pillar of strength (Annapolis 1920, and the only regular Navy man with continuous

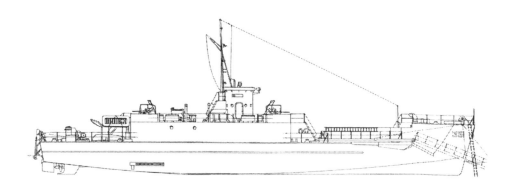

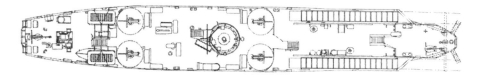

Landing Craft Infantry Large, LCI L, used to land 200 infantry
directly onto beaches. *A.D. Baker*

LCI L specifications:
    Length: 158 ft.
    Beam: 23 ft.
    Draft: unloaded 2' 8" in forward, 4' 10" in aft
    Speed: 16 knots (max.)
    Ship complement: 4 officers and 24 enlisted men
    Troop complement: 6 officers and 200 enlisted men
    Cargo capacity: 75 tons
    Endurance: 4,000 mile cruise distance steaming at 12 knots
    Armament: Five 20mm guns
    Fuel: 130 tons
    Propulsion: Two sets of 4 GM diesels, twin propellers

service in our staff and officer group), very easy to work with, but a damn good disciplinarian and leader."

Walton's flotilla consisted of three groups of 12 LCIs. In a letter to May, Jannotta described the LCIs as "sweet little ships". But the crews were another matter. Some had been standing by at the shipyard for two weeks waiting for the launch of their ship. "No Naval quarters, no Naval mess facilities, no pay, no instruction, no nothing. Was their morale low!" Jannotta wrote. And to top it off there was not a single experienced enlisted man or officer. The enlisted men, just out of boot camp, had to be made into boatswains' mates, gunners, helmsmen, radio men, signal men, engineers, and machinist mates in two to three months' time. Not a single officer had sea or ship handling experience.

Over the following weeks, Jannotta took delivery of additional LCIs from Galveston's Brown Shipyard. His approach to training his ship captains and crews was straightforward. "I take each one out myself twice (two days)—and then dump it right in the skipper's lap from there on to handle. While we're out I get them (officers and each individual crew man) instructed in ship handling." For two months straight, the flotilla ran through maneuvers, constantly practicing in all conditions, slowly growing in competence and confidence.

In late December, Jannotta departed Galveston for the South Pacific. "My flagship was designated as the guide," he wrote to May, explaining that this meant "my ship is at the head and center, and all other ships keep station on me. We have 45 ships in our convoy—36 LCIs, 2 LSTs (Landing Ship Tanks) and 7 escorts—sub-chasers. They make a pretty sight—6 columns of 6—1 LST on each flank, 3 destroyers ranging out in front, and 2 on each flank."

Crossing the Pacific was not without moments of tension. During one particularly stormy night, an LST with a jammed rudder came within yards of taking out Jannotta's LCI, but didn't due to his quick thinking and maneuvering. "The damn fool ran half through our convoy. Over a third of our ships were scattered all over the horizon."

When the convoy sailed into Noumea, New Caledonia, in early April he proudly proclaimed their 9,000-mile voyage an accomplishment. "We started with newly commissioned and outfitted ships, the designs and engines of which had never been proven before, and with every officer and man without any previous Naval or sea experience. The ships, the officers, the men, have met the test beautifully." A remarkable voyage considering the LCI L was about the size of Christopher Columbus' *Santa Maria*.

At Noumea, the site of 3rd Fleet Headquarters and Admiral William F. Halsey's command post, combat preparations for Amphibious Forces intensified. Jannotta had kept up a relentless work schedule commissioning ships and training crews at Galveston, but life at Noumea was even more demanding. His days started at 5:30 a.m. and ended around midnight. "I'm pushing every minute," he told May. Over the next two months, the LCI officers and crews focused on simulating landing troops onto island beaches. It involved an innovative technique: as the LCI approached its landing, a stern anchor was dropped and played out until the ship nudged into the shore, in as little as three feet of water. Then, 28' port and starboard ramps, just aft of the bow, were lowered to discharge the troops. Once men and material were ashore, the engine was reversed while the stern anchor was winched in until the ship was free floating.

On June 21, 1943, Jannotta and his men shipped out for Guadalcanal, now the center of Allied fleet action, to join Admiral Halsey's 3rd Fleet. It was in final preparation for an attack in the middle Solomon Islands of Rendova and New Georgia, a massive operation dubbed "Toenails." It included 5 aircraft carriers, 5 battleships, 4 light cruisers, 32 destroyers and upwards of 100 amphibious ships and landing craft. The primary objective was to take the Japanese airfield at Munda, on New Georgia Island, five miles northeast across the channel from Rendova. Capturing Munda would provide the Allies a forward base from which to launch bombing runs on Japanese positions on or near Bougainville (where Kawanishi was scheduled to arrive in three weeks). For Jannotta and his LCI L group it would be the first test under fire. That day came on July 2. A week later, Jannotta put the experience to paper.

My Sweetheart,
So much has happened, and events have been moving so very fast since I wrote you before leaving

50

Guadalcanal! I left there the night of July 2 with 13 LCI Ls under my command to go up with troops on our first combat operation. At Russell Islands, while I was loading troops, Admiral Forte sped alongside in a PT boat and personally gave me orders to include four LSTs in my Task Unit and, after making our assault landings, to send the LSTs back to Guadalcanal, but to stay up there myself with six of my LCI Ls to serve under the commander of assault forces. I had infantry aboard the LCI Ls, artillery aboard the LSTs—17 ships and about 4,000 troops. I got them all loaded and the CO's all briefed just before dark of the 3rd. Shoved off, formed up in a blinding rain, and set course and speed to rendezvous at 1930 with two destroyers Admiral Forte had assigned to me for escort. Arrived at the latitude and longitude of rendezvous on time, and no destroyers. Slowed down the formation and cruised around a large circle, but no destroyers. They never did show up. Well, I couldn't turn back because my orders were positive—I had to have my ships at Rendova the next morning, the 4th, ready to start putting the troops on the beaches at 0700. Though Jap subs patrolled the 120 miles of waters through which I had to go, and Jap land forces held all the islands between and around which I had to pass, and I had no protection for my ships or forces on them, I knew I had no choice but to take the risks and go ahead.

God, what a night that was! You couldn't see a thing—low, black clouds and a heavy curtain of rain shut down the visibility to less than 200 yards. I had my ships in two columns behind me—mine in the center, leading eight ships to a column on each side of me. Could only see one ship in column, all night. I laid my course to play safe going around reefs and islands, which were all enemy held and poorly charted, but had to guess at our drift from wind and current and the speed we were making good. Couldn't and didn't see all night a damn land mass we could take a sight on, identify, and check our position. Just had to pray

Jannotta's flagship USS *LCI L 328* and USS *LCI L 336* bringing materials ashore at Rendova in the Solomon Islands. July 4, 1943. *US Navy*

I was guessing my course and speeds closely enough so I would not pile my ships on reefs or islands which we would not have been able to see soon enough to avoid, if I were wrong. The responsibility was mine, and mine alone, as to whether we got through, or piled up, and I surely did some hard figuring on all the alternative possibilities of where our position might be at given times, and some tall finger-crossing, came dawn and we were due to see something in the way of land.

We did make our landfalls right on the nose, at daybreak. Believe me, it was a great relief to finally identify and take bearings on certain land masses that proved I was where I thought I was, and was supposed to be. I had to change course several times during the night, too, and I really prayed that the ships were keeping close up and would follow the ship ahead, and be with me in the morning. That was quite a thrill and a great tribute to the ships' officers to finally, at dawn, count the ships up and find them all present.

We got quite a reception when we got here—from enemy planes and shore forces—but we're now well entrenched and are getting wonderful air coverage from our air fields a long way back.

Our troops have pretty well cleaned the Japs out on the island (Rendova) and we are now landing troops each day on the one across the way (New Georgia). There are about four miles of water between the two—mostly reefs.

Since the first day we reached here, when three of my ships (the 23, 24 and 66) were hit and badly damaged, and we had a number of casualties, I've had no more casualties. We lay up in coves against the jungle and put camouflage over our ships to make them inconspicuous as possible in the daytime when we're not on the move on mission. We communicate by radio and are on alert all the time, and at battle stations several times a day or night, waiting (to fight off) air attacks.

Have had to go ashore on three or four occasions to report or get orders in person that couldn't be transmitted by radio from commander of assault forces, and believe me, I'll take the water any day. This country is beautiful—mountainous and covered with green foliage, but the jungle is lousy, full of ants, mosquitoes, and slimy mucky mud. Have been caught twice during air raids; had to lie in a water-filled foxhole for an hour one time, and in thick mud under a truck with five other unrecognizable men for an hour and a half the second time. Couldn't see a darned thing—just listen, wait and pray. No, I'll take the good clean deck on a ship, the salt air, and the freedom of movement of a ship at sea. How these boys in the Army and Marines stand it ashore, I don't know. It rains often, and the jungle is smothering, fetid and unclean, and they're wet and muddy practically all the time. Believe me, my hat's off to them.

But then, every one of these men and boys out here—Navy afloat, in small boats, or ashore; Seabees (Naval Construction Battalion personnel), Marines, and Army—is a hero. They take it all in their stride, and work and fight like hell. Hours mean nothing to anybody. I've been up 60 hours straight without a wink; others have and do go longer. Men being killed and messed up all around is taken most stoically and casually. It has to be, or they'd go nuts. I find myself getting that way, too, and I'm glad I do. I don't like to think back on how I felt when I buried and said a few words over the first three of my own boys who were killed—with just a long trench hurriedly scooped out of the jungle mud by a bulldozer for a grave for them, and numberless others.

We're getting fine planes out here, though pitifully few, and our American boys and the New Zealanders are real fighters—vastly superior to the Japs. But he's got so much more than we have—and he's a tough fighter who doesn't know when he's licked—and he'll make suicide attacks or commit suicide before he'll quit. So nobody here feels that what we are up against is going to be anything but a long, tough grind, to win through.

I am perfectly well, and physically in good shape. We still eat regularly, though we're getting low on food and water, and hope it won't be long before they get a provision ship up to us. We don't have a chance to sleep much, but we're managing to get along all right.

All my love, Sweetheart.
Vernon

Jannotta's actions on July 3-6 didn't go unnoticed: Admiral Halsey awarded him the Bronze Star. The citation indicated that while his LCI Ls were disembarking troops, the ships were attacked by 16 enemy bombers in low-level runs. The anti-aircraft fire from his ships knocked down six bombers; however, in the mêlée, three of his ships were hit and badly damaged. Jannotta quickly moved to their aid, removing the dead and caring for the wounded, and then personally directed the salvage work. Within a short time, the ships were made seaworthy. In the air attack on July 4, Jannotta received several shrapnel wounds himself but continued to exercise command. For the wounds, he was awarded the Purple Heart.

That successful rescue of men and ships was the first of several instances when physical courage played an important role in his actions as a leader.

USS *LCI L 328* at Rendova in the Solomon Islands, July 4, 1943. *US Navy*

A P-40 Fighter protects the landing of American troops on the island of Rendova in the Solomon Islands, June 30, 1943. *US Navy*

Chapter VII
THE AIR WAR

COSTLY ALLIED VICTORIES OF GUADALCANAL AND MUNDA

In all, operations to take the middle Solomon Islands proved less bloody than the Battle for Guadalcanal, but the invasions of Rendova and Munda were still costly. At Munda, 1,136 Army and Marine ground forces were killed (compared to 1,592 at Guadalcanal). For the Japanese, however, the toll was severe; an estimated 10,000 died on Munda. In an August 18 letter to his wife, Jannotta, after a thorough tour of the battlefield, recorded his impressions of the fight:

> The entire area—from the beach on a front of four or five miles north and east of Munda Point (where the airstrip starts), back into the jungles on every hill for a depth of several miles—was literally honeycombed with an elaborate, interlacing system of pill-boxes, gun emplacements and dugouts. They didn't throw them up after we had landed, or in a few days before we attacked. They were planned and built over a period of months.
>
> Pillboxes and dugouts had walls and roofs from five to as much as ten feet thickness of coral, concrete and logs. All the large dugouts were dug deep into the hills with dozens of feet of earth above. No wonder the Japs could take the terrific bombings I saw them given day after day

for four weeks straight. It wasn't their numbers, nor their vaunted fighting ability as individual soldiers, that made the battle of Munda tough and longer than we expected—it was their defense system of pill boxes, gun emplacements and dugouts. Our casualties have been plenty—but I can understand why, after seeing what our troops were up against. In terms of the strength of the Jap defenses and the strategic importance of the Munda Airfield, our losses were low and, in comparison with the Jap losses, very low. He lost many thousands—killed—we have very few prisoners.

"The shame of surrender was burned deeply in the consciousness of the Japanese," wrote anthropologist Ruth Benedict. Their honor was tied to dying rather than laying down their arms. When taken as a prisoner, even if wounded and unconscious, a soldier was disgraced and dead to his former life. When Admiral John S. McCain, Sr. was decorated for rescuing two damaged American warships, the Japanese radio had this to say, "We are not questioning the veracity of Admiral McCain's rescuing two ships, but the point we want you to see is the curious fact that the rescuing of damaged ships merits decoration in the United States." Japanese valor did not include salvaging. The use of parachutes, for instance, raised the cry of cowardice. Death in battle was the triumph of the spirit, and in itself, heroic.

Due to the tenacious resolve of the Japanese soldier and his defense systems, it took the US and its Allies 84 days to achieve victory at Munda and five months at Guadalcanal. By simple projections these figures pushed the defeat of Japan far into the future and beyond the patience of its military leaders—Admirals King, Nimitz and Halsey, and General MacArthur—prompting these men to initiate a major strategic change.

Early in 1943, Admiral Yamamoto promised Emperor Hirohito to avenge the loss of Guadalcanal with a counter-offensive in the Solomon Islands. The plan called for an overwhelming air offensive against Allied bases on Guadalcanal. To implement the attack, Yamamoto concentrated close to 400 fighters and medium-range bombers in the northern Solomons.

The air offensive was crucial to Japanese strategy for several reasons. First, Japan needed to protect Rabaul. Located on New Britain Island more than 600 miles northwest of Guadalcanal, Rabaul was Japan's biggest South Pacific port. Rabaul boasted a perfectly shaped harbor with enough anchorage for a vast fleet. It bustled with 100,000 troops and support personnel and was ringed by five airfields. The Imperial Japanese Navy 3rd Fleet's four aircraft carriers and dozens of cruisers and destroyers moved in and out of Rabaul. It was the ideal spot from which to both launch and defend attacks. Scores of naval and air assaults against Allied forces in the Solomons came from here, and more than half the aircraft in the Munda counter-offensive took off from the airfields around Rabaul. Second, the port had to be defended: it was the strategic linchpin protecting Japanese held territory further west in the Philippines and the oil-rich Dutch East Indies.

To support the counterattack, Japanese commanders also poured materials and men (including Ensign Kawanishi) into Buin, Bougainville. Among the offensive capabilities were carrier-based Aichi 99 dive-bombers. An Aichi 99 leaving Buin for an attack on Rendova could make the 100-mile crossing in less than 45 minutes. As soon as the Japanese bombers beeped onto Allied radar, antiaircraft guns and fighter planes jumped to life. In the amphibious fleet, Lieutenant Commander Vernon Jannotta and his men, moored in jungle-lined coves at Rendova, would scramble to wait it out at battle stations.

Rendova, August 7, 1943

My Sweetheart,

At 1515, we received our "daily" radio warning of enemy planes approaching, and went to battle stations. Our scout planes, or radar equipment ashore, pick up the planes 50 or 60 miles away, usually. That gives us 10 to 15 minutes advance notice if they come right in. But usually they don't—they circle around so as to approach from some unexpected quarter—and always way above the clouds and out of sight until they're ready to attack. Our fighters go milling around the clouds trying to find them to break them up. Most of the time they do—but sometimes they'll get fooled by the Jap fighters leading them away from the bombers—or all the bombers get through and have all the time they want to pick their targets and make their runs.

Well, that happened today. Twenty minutes after having been tensely waiting at battle stations we finally heard them, out of sight above the clouds (the sky was full of clouds overhead today) at about 1535. Then at 1540, we saw a flock of Jap fighters break through the clouds heading away from Rendova. Our fighters followed. Then we heard the fighters "dog fighting" in the clouds ahead and to the right of us. At about 1545, we saw bomber after bomber appear out of the clouds in succession (they were all dive bombers today—Aichi 99s) diving for targets in and around the harbor—saw the ack ack fire spotting up from all ships; saw and heard the explosions of the bombs—around shore installations and a couple of our ships some distance away, all out of range of our ship guns. We were nervous, fascinated spectators, but not participants.

Then, suddenly, the picture changed. One of the Japs apparently spotted us. I had three of my LCI Ls beached in a cove together, 50 to 60 feet apart, taking on fresh water from one of the streams—the 328, 336 and 66. My flagship, the 328, was in the center—66 on our right, 336 on our left. He was about 6,000 feet up and a couple of miles dead ahead of us, heading with others for the other end of Rendova Harbor. He banked and started coming straight down at us. This was about 1549. A few seconds later, all 20mms on all three ships opened up on him. He kept coming and was now heading from dead ahead of us, right for the 328—the center ship.

The tracers from our guns were pouring all around him, and into him, and I remember thinking, "Why doesn't that b____ fall?" By some miracle he didn't. In a few seconds, he was within a hundred feet of the surface and a couple of hundred feet dead ahead—coming like a bat out of hell right straight at us on the 328. All ships were still pouring right into him—our machine guns were also firing now. I thought, "Well, this is it." In another second, he leveled at about 50 feet above us, and I saw his bombs fly out—three of them, one big and two small. His plane sort of slipped a little to our left—the bombs seeming to slide off to our right. He flashed right over my head—I was on the conning station, and I remember registering seeing several holes in his wings—one seemed almost two feet in diameter, and he was smoking, heavy, black smoke. Then, the explosions. This was at 1551. They were something. The ship lifted up, and then, for what seemed ages, but was probably only a few seconds, water, sand, mud, and coral poured down on us in the conn—we were 26 feet above the water—in such volume and force that it literally beat us down to the deck.

I picked myself up and scrambled to the starboard side of the conn to see what had happened to our own ship and the 66—the bombs had missed the 328 and had landed in the water between us and the 66, just forward of the conning station. I fully expected to see our bow, and 66's bow, blown with plenty of holes below the waterline as well as above, and the gunners stretched out who were on the No. 1 gun of each ship—located in the nose of the ship.

Well, to even up the miracle of the Jap getting through our fire to release his bombs where he judged he'd get us, another miracle had happened. Neither the 66 nor the 328 had any holes of any consequence in her hull—not a man had been killed or seriously wounded (three boys on the 328 had superficial flesh wounds from shrapnel). I still can't get over the wonder of it. The answer is that in this particular cove, where we were beached to take on water, the stream had washed a very deep bed of mud and sand over the hard coral bottom, and this enabled the bombs to go deep enough in the soft sandy mud, before exploding, to smother the spread of the shrapnel and the force of water concussion.

When just one bomb—not three—landed between the 24 and 66 on July 4, it just absolutely shredded the hulls of the two ships—below and above the water line—one hole in the 66 was four feet by eight feet, half of it below the water line—and killed three and seriously wounded six men. Here, three bombs had landed between two ships, with no serious damage and only three minor casualties.

The 66 had her port ramp (weighing 3,500 lbs.) tossed in the air, twisted into scrap, and blown into the water—but not a single shrapnel hole and no other damage. We had perhaps a dozen shrapnel holes into my cabin, the pilot house, and the conning station, which are above each other in reverse order; our compass on the conn was blown out; our radio antennae, signal halyards, etc., were shredded; our battle lights, glassware and china in various compartments knocked off and spread around; shrapnel pieces all over the deck—and that was all—nothing serious. All of which proves we were damn lucky. That's what it's like to be attacked by a dive-bomber. And if anyone describes the experience with enthusiasm and says it's "fun"—you put him down as a damned liar, or completely nuts. You don't have a chance to be scared while he's diving at you and before his bombs hit—it's happening too fast and you're concentrating on the effort to get him before he gets you. But—when it's over—then your heart really pounds, and you sweat, thinking about it.

We stayed at battle stations for another 15 or 20 minutes after that as there were still other planes around us but eventually, they had unloaded their bombs and left us. We "secured".

Then everybody started laughing and hollering—all talking at once—the reaction.

Oh, we feel pretty sure we got the Jap. He didn't crash within sight of us, but many men testify that his wings and fuselage were literally full of holes—he was smoking and he didn't zoom up to get altitude again after releasing his

The Aichi D3A1 (Val) went into service as the Navy Type 99 Model 11 carrier dive bomber of the Imperial Japanese Navy (IJN).

bombs, as they always do—he kept going, dead astern of us, only 30 to 40 feet above the water, until a coral reef a few feet out of water about two miles astern of us, and the haze of a cloudy day, lost him to sight. It doesn't seem possible that he could have made it home. But, since we didn't see him hit the water, we can't claim a "sure"—we can only claim a "probable" kill.

He was an "Aichi 99"—one of the Jap crack dive-bombers—carrier-based.

I'll have to send the 66 back to Guadalcanal to get a new ramp and equipment made—and get another ship up here to replace it. I'm evacuating a youngster from 327 on it at the same time. These bombings have broken his nerve, and for the past week, he's been shaking and ready to break. He tries—and he's afraid of going hysterical in front of the other men—but he can't help himself. This is the first one I've had in my outfit, though I've seen many others (Army mostly) being shipped back for the same reason.

The morale and courage of these youngsters on these ships are really wonderful. They feel fear, just as I do, I'm sure, but they hide it under a smiling, wise-cracking, tall storytelling front that's good to see and hear.

I'm anxious to hear from you.

Goodnight, my Sweetheart, and worlds and worlds of love.

Vernon

Just as at Midway, air combat didn't play out according to Japanese theory. A number of factors intervened. One was the introduction of new Allied aircraft. In February 1943, a Marine fighter squadron introduced the high-powered and heavily armed F4U Corsair at Henderson Field at Guadalcanal. It flew faster and higher than the Zero, and outclimbed it. At about the same time, the Army brought to the theater its high performance, twin-engine and -tailed P-38 Lightning. At first, the numbers of these planes were small. In March 1943, the Marines had just 2 fighter squadrons of 16 F4Us and 24 pilots. But by June, 8 more Marine squadrons were operational—and devastating. One Marine squadron, VMF 124, was credited with 68 victories while losing just 11 F4Us and 7 pilots to combat and 4 to accidents.*

Even as US planes improved, Japan stayed with the same planes it had flown at the start of the war. Unlike Allied aircraft, these planes lacked self-sealing gas tanks and, when hit, became fireballs. Furthermore, downed Japanese pilots were most often left unrescued, indoctrinated to die rather than surrender. By contrast, the Allies made every effort to save their pilots. A final factor in the air war was training. The US sent combat-experienced aviators home to train green pilots, and for rest and recuperation. It ensured a flow of proficient aviators as its air fleet expanded and underpinned pilot morale. By contrast, Japanese squadrons were often kept in combat until they were wiped out, and replacement pilots were greener and younger with every passing battle.

Both Jannotta and Kawanishi gave their observations of the air war. Jannotta made his in an April 25, 1943 letter:

---

*Bartlett Tillman. *Corsair, The F4U in World War II and Korea* (Annapolis, US Naval Institute, 1979)

...(the) surprising thing is the small number of our planes that we've lost—both in the daily Jap raids on Rendova Harbor and our raids over Munda. We've never seen more than one or two of our planes go down in any one action, and many days none at all. Of course, we can't see everything— but we do see most—and it's real satisfying that our boys are really "dishing it out" with very small loss. Every time we see one of our planes start smoking and falling, we also see a parachute bloom out, and we've picked up three of these shot-down fliers ourselves; the regular crash boat several others. We've never seen a Jap flier use a parachute. Apparently, the story is true that they are not provided with them. Result; every time the Japs lose a plane, they lose the pilot and the crew. Much of the time that we lose planes, we do not lose the pilot. So the ratio of Jap air losses to ours, which MacArthur claims is seven to our one plane, and which, in this area, has certainly been at least that—is even greater in the matter of pilots.

Reflecting on the air war, Kawanishi recorded these observations in a September diary entry:

We could do nothing but watch the dogfights above us. Our squadrons lost pilots every day throughout the war of attrition. And yet, though they took to the air as if they were on their way to meet death, their spirits never flagged in the slightest. Their valiant effort utterly convinced me that it was this spirit that made the Japanese military strong.

But no matter how many enemy planes fell to the ground, their numbers increased, while ours steadily dwindled. The numerical advantage gradually tipped in their favor. Initially, the enemy attacked only once in the morning, but in time, they began to launch further air raids in the afternoon. Attrition had reduced our planes to about 30, and rather than risk total annihilation, they withdrew to Rabaul.

LSTs approaching Rendova, July 1943. *US Navy*

Chapter VIII
GRANDPA!

In a 1943 letter to May, Jannotta complained:

> It seems ages since I've had a letter from you, though actually, I presume, it's about two weeks.

Not a man to grouse, Jannotta was grousing. Mail, news from home, like breathing, was basic to Jannotta's well being. It connected him to loved ones. So when Jannotta discovered one of his "loved ones" on Guadalcanal, the encounter had to have been extraordinary:

> *USS* LCI L 328
> August 29, 1943, Florida Is., Solomons
>
> My Sweetheart,
>   The last three or four days have certainly been eventful ones for me. I found Nick (son-in-law and Marine Captain Henry Nickel) and received word about the baby. Isn't that an amazing coincidence, that both should happen at the same time?
>   It was from Nick that I first learned about the baby and that it was a boy, named Henry Vernon, weighing close to seven pounds, born on August 8, and that Shirley and the youngster are OK— Of course I'm "Grandpa" now to all.

Some 11,000 miles from home and family, fighting in a brutal war, it's not surprising Nick and Vernon were thrilled to see each other; besides, the two men had a special relationship. With only daughters, Vernon thought of Nick as his son; in return Nick admired his father-in-law, enjoyed his company, and looked upon him as a close friend. Over hard–to-find beer, they toasted the baby and the mother, and during the next day, they spent intense moments catching up, first at Nick's outfit and then on board Jannotta's LCI L. Jannotta summed up the occurrence:

> I think he enjoyed the day and found it interesting. I know I did—it was a most eventful twenty-four hours for me to see him and be with him.

> *USS* LCI L 328
> October 8, 1943, Florida Is., Solomons

> My Darling Girl,
>   Received your letter a couple of days ago. It was a grand letter—so long and so full of news. I've read it over a dozen times.
>   Life out here continues its strange pattern of quick and unexpected change from inactivity and deadly monotony to strenuous activity and movement, to suspense and tension of action, and then back again. Another offensive is in the making and we are getting ready for it—overhauling machinery, equipment, guns; daily drills and tactical exercises; frequent exercises with troops—in between the jobs of taking in new troops or reinforcements regularly to Munda, Vella Lavella, and, just recently, to Kolombangara.

But in a November 8 letter to May, the preparation for combat picked-up:

> We've been pretty much on the go ourselves this past couple of weeks and will be busy constantly for the next few months

now, thank goodness. I leave in the morning with my ships for the start of the show, which you'll undoubtedly read something about even before you get this letter. Everyone is relieved that the period of marking time—as we've been doing more or less for the past couple of months—is over, and is eager to get going.

Just lost another of my commanding officers for return to the States for new construction (new ships are being turned out awfully fast there now, and the forces afloat all have to contribute personnel to man them).

Jannotta was referring to the Navy's ramp-up of men and ships for future landings in the Pacific and for D-day at Normandy, France.

USS LCI L 328
November 8, 1943, Guadalcanal

My Sweetheart,

We're on the offensive again. I presume you've been getting the reports of our landings at Treasury Island and Bougainville, the bombings of Rabaul and our fleet actions at sea. The radio broadcasts from US don't exaggerate a bit. We've been giving the Japs hell on land, sea, and air. We've completed the capture of Treasury Island, and cleaned out the Japs there—we're well entrenched at Bougainville and have already knocked out most of their airfields there and at Shortlands. We've been knocking off their planes on a ratio of better than ten to one, and we've sunk plenty of cruisers, destroyers, cargo vessels, and landing craft. The last sea action, a few days ago, we sank two cruisers and four destroyers, and damaged four others—and did not lose a single ship of ours.

When we went into Treasury Islands, we hit it at dawn—the destroyers lying off shore about three miles shelling Jap artillery positions—LCI Ls racing in to the beaches—LSTs following—we all went in firing everything we had, raking machine gun nests, and trees for snipers, along the shore—it reminded me of the stories of the wild west with crazy cowboys riding into town with all guns blazing. Our troops got off in a good time, and although you could hear bullets whistling past for several minutes, and Jap mortar shells were exploding ahead and behind us, our LCI Ls didn't have a single casualty. We had 10 LCIs on that landing (5 of my group and 5 of Rear Admiral Richard E. Byrd's. Two of the LSTs got hit badly (mortar fire) and later, when dive-bombers attacked, one of the destroyers was hit—but none sank.

It was a beautifully planned and executed affair. Within an hour we had the beachhead established—and the Japs on the run into the mountains—and before the afternoon was over the last Jap battery had been knocked out. We had marvelous air coverage (fighters) over us, too—and mine sweeps preceded us into the harbor to clear mines from our path. We caught the Japs off guard, and they didn't get any effective land or air attacks going until the following day.

Bougainville was the same story, on a much larger scale. The Japs gave us more intensive and larger attacks and sent a task force against us by sea. Our ships and planes knocked the hell out of the Jap planes and our own task force sank five Jap warships and chased the rest away. Our casualties—ships, planes, men, have so far been amazingly small.

One of our LCIs had the most miraculous experience the other night. It and an MTB (Motor Torpedo Boat) were escorting a LCT (Landing Craft Tank) from Treasury to Bougainville when a formation of 12 Jap torpedo planes attacked them (about 1945 at night, just after dark). But the LCI and the MTB were torpedoed. The MTB had its bow cut off, but the torpedo didn't explode. The LCI was hit in the engine room—the torpedo is still in the engine room, unexploded. (850 lbs. of TNT in that torpedo would have blown the ship so wide apart we wouldn't have found any pieces). Only one boy was killed (in the engine room)—no other casualties, and both the LCI and MTB were safely towed into Bougainville. The LCIs have been credited with shooting down 6 of the Jap planes and the MTB with one—they got 7 out of 12 of the planes. Pretty good, and pretty lucky!! The LCIers "live right", as they say.

We're loading now at Guadalcanal—New Zealand combat units for Treasury Island reinforcements—I have six LCIs with me on this trip. When we've landed our troops I'm taking the 328 to Bougainville to tow the 70 (the one that has the torpedo in it) back to Guadalcanal for repairs.

Besides taking assault troops to capture beachheads, we take in reinforcements, shift units from one flank to another, and sometimes evacuate them. We had one of these latter assignments the other night. A large force of Marine paratroopers had landed at a certain spot on Choiseul Island as a diversionary force—to fool the Jap to where we were putting in other main forces—with orders to hold their position for one week, and then they would be evacuated. This bunch—about 1,700—fooled them so well the Japs rushed in about 5,000 men (from Bougainville) around them.

The paratroopers (Lieutenant Colonel (LCOL) Victor H. "Brute" Krulak's 2nd Parachute Battalion, 1st Marine Amphibious Corps) held their positions for four days—by which time our main landings had been successfully effected at Treasury and Bougainville, and the Japs had our paratroopers surrounded and so badly pressed that Corps headquarters wanted to get them out pronto. Three of our LCIs were handed the job. (Two of my group, one from Byrd's) It had to be done at night to avoid the ships being shelled and the troops massacred in the process of loading. They fought their way down to a narrow strip of beach — about 500 yards wide—and our ships had to find their way into this and be there at midnight. We arranged a series of flashlight signals to identify our own troops—stayed in hiding in a cove on the northern coast of Vella Lavella in the afternoon and started after dark for this spot on the map on Choiseul.

The shore, jungle and mountains all merged into one black mass, and you couldn't make out a thing on shore. We saw a flashing light and started for it, but headed away again when a re-check of our courses, speed and time indicated that we were still about 10 miles from the part of the coast we wanted to hit. Lucky, too. It wasn't our fellows.

We finally sneaked in close to shore—ran along for about eight miles at full speed, and they saw our lights. We went in—beached—fortunately no reefs or rocks—and were they glad to see us!!! They piled on in a hurry, with equipment and casualties—and we were off and on our way in half an hour. Not a single shot was fired at us. Even so, we all heaved a big sign of relief when we were out to sea again. We got about 650 out on that trip.

Am sending with this a copy of my "Officer Qualifications Questionnaire" which I would like to keep because of the comments my flotilla commander, Commander Smith, put on it. Frankly, I was surprised and delighted, because I didn't think he'd ever have a good word to say for anybody (he rides the hell out of all of us), and the commands for which he recommends me can only be held by 3-stripers (CDR)—not a 2 1/2 striper (LCDR).

Our LCIs have been doing a wonderful job these past five months—and today we have the respect and admiration of the most crusty and skeptical—cruiser, destroyer and transport commands, and staff, from Admiral William Frederick Halsey, Jr., down. I think they're the greatest bunch of guys—of brain and men—ever put together. They can do anything that's batted up to them—they haven't failed to successfully complete every single mission handed them.

I have to get along now. Will write again soon.
Worlds of love, Darling.

LSTs loading, Guadalcanal, 1943. *US Navy*

Torpedo boat sailors take a rest. *US Navy*

Chapter IX
ALLIED TASK FORCE FORMS AND HEADS NORTH

NOVEMBER 1943, BUIN, BOUGAINVILLE

By November 1943, the battles for Rendova, Munda and Kolombangara were over. Overwhelming enemy air, sea and ground forces pushed back the drastically under-supplied and -manned Japanese forces. Ultimately, Japanese units on the northern end of Kolombangara withdrew to Choiseul Island to its north and from there to Bougainville. Executing the withdrawal fell to Kawanishi and his supply officers and men. It was "extremely difficult", penned Kawanishi:

> *Enemy PT boats and destroyers constantly patrolled the straits between Kolombangara and Choiseul. The enemy also attacked from the air. But our plan to secretly withdraw under cover of darkness met with good fortune. Using only a few destroyers, we successfully withdrew with only minor resistance from enemy ships because they had turned their attention to the southern side of the island where most of the fighting was taking place. Though most of the personnel there had perished during months of fighting, we nonetheless managed to withdraw and consolidate the fraction of the 8th Combined Special Landing Group that had survived.*

While accomplishing a total withdrawal is nothing to be proud of, succeeding at such a terribly difficult operation put our headquarters in an ebullient mood, something that it hadn't experienced in a long time.

Meanwhile, the calm that had prevailed for a time over Bougainville came to an end. In mid-November, daily reconnaissance flights from Rabaul began reporting a drastic increase in the number of enemy transports anchored at Lungga on Guadalcanal. They observed 20, then 30, transports along with 15 cruiser and destroyer escorts. The flotilla swelled to 70 vessels. The build-up continued until it exceeded the moorings at Lungga and spilled out onto the open sea, then it headed north. The normal period between Allied island landings was three to four months—the time it took for Allied ships, men and materials to assemble. But this time there was no breathing spell. The event pointed to the US's and Allies' building their operational capability. Kawanishi wrote:

Even as the massive flotilla headed northward under cover of countless aerial and naval escorts, we didn't know where it would land—Shortland Island to the south of Bougainville or Buin where the main Japanese force was deployed. We had no aircraft capable of mounting a counterattack. We could only sit and wait for an attack that would come sometime between the night and morning of November 22-23, 1943.

The flotilla steadily moved toward land. Headquarters, though tense, was prepared for what lay ahead. We had no choice but to fight without having finished settling in after our withdrawal from Kolombangara and with defensive preparations only partly completed. During the day, headquarters was busy giving orders to all the units in the area, but by evening things had calmed down a bit. I went back to our barracks and took a hot bath to purify myself. When the time came, I wanted to die like a true warrior.

We had a bath in the jungle made from an oil drum

placed on a floor of sticks and twigs and covered by a thatched roof. When I sank down into the hot water, my head filled with thoughts of my school days and other memories of home. I felt at peace. I even hummed to myself a few songs from home. As I shaved, I thought that even though 23 years isn't very long, I'd lived a pretty full life.

After I got out of the bath, I put on my jungle camouflage fatigues, which I had been saving for the right occasion, instead of my usual summer uniform. My mood turned solemn as I put on this uniform for the first time. I strapped my saber around my waist and went to headquarters.

When Kawanishi entered headquarters, he was greeted with, "Hey, you're ready to go. You look pretty good in a land uniform." Others in the room shouted and joked with him. When Kawanishi joined the officers in the operations room, they toasted with *sake* to their success in the coming battle. Normally late-night talk focused on the day's casualties and which of Buin's facilities had been damaged or destroyed in the day's air raids. But on this night the discussion never strayed far from what the next day would bring. As the night passed, Kawanishi and the others waited for updates on the movements of the American invasion fleet. During the previous day, the patrol pilots had seen more than 100 ships sailing north through the central Solomons. Despite the somber situation, Kawanishi and the other officers drank and wished each other well and quietly waited for their orders.

In the early morning hours, the news finally filtered through camp—the American fleet had snuck west around the Treasury Islands and landed its troops at a lightly defended area well up Bougainville's west coast at Empress Bay. Kawanishi took off his battle fatigues. His disappointment was palpable and he wrote so in his journal. Now the enemy had avoided a battle by landing at Empress Bay and was protected by 80 miles of thick jungle that separated the enemy and Japanese forces at Buin.

"Now what?" Kawanishi must have wondered.

Bougainville. *US Navy*

Chapter X

THE BATTLE FOR BOUGAINVILLE

NOVEMBER 1943

Kawanishi and Jannotta never met in person, or directly on the battlefield, but they both fought on Bougainville Island. Neither was involved in the Allies' initial landings, which were masterpieces of diversion; Kawanishi and the rest of the main Japanese force were completely bypassed when the US Marines landed in the middle of Bougainville at Empress Bay, rather than the south, where they'd been expected. While Kawanishi, wearing an army-style uniform, was waiting in vain for the attack that never came, Jannotta had participated in the deception that helped make the Bougainville landings successful. In particular, he had snuck Lieutenant Colonel Krulak's group of hardened Marines off Choiseul Island, from their diversionary action there, and was now several weeks later transporting them to Bougainville.

USS LCI L 328
November 24, 1943, At Sea, So. Pacific

My Sweetheart,
    We first landed in the Treasury Islands, as you know, on Oct. 27—that was quite a show. I've been on three missions there, and the capture and occupation of these is now complete. We hit Bougainville, in the central section

(Empress Augusta Bay) on Nov. 1 and have gradually been extending, reinforcing and consolidating our position there since. There are still about 30,000 Japs on Bougainville—southeast and northwest of our positions—so it will take a while yet, with some tough fighting, before we have completed the job there. I can't describe or discuss the tactical strategy used and to be used here, but it's good—and things are moving along according to schedule...

The 1943 Japanese strategy called for stockpiling Rabaul as a central bastion so that it could supply men and munitions to Bougainville as well as other islands in the Solomon Island chain. By deploying the tenacious Japanese foot soldier in the path of the island-hopping Allies, the goal was to wear down and frustrate the offense. Given that it had taken the Allies six months to secure Guadalcanal, by a quick calculation, it could take US forces more than a year to reach Rabaul. However, Admiral Halsey's staff, with the help and support of Admiral Nimitz and General MacArthur, developed their own tactic: leapfrog past key Japanese military bases, leaving these units to wither on the vine. As it turned out, it was a fate that Kawanishi and 30,000 Japanese troops faced at Buin, Bougainville. Moreover, the US Navy's operational capability in the sea and air by late 1943 was strong enough to ensure the leapfrogging strategy's success. Jannotta wrote:

At the moment, I'm on a mission with six of our LCI Ls to Bougainville. This one is more or less typical. On the night of the 20th a large number of us are on shore from LCIs anchored or beached in the harbor near our base on Florida Island, taking in a movie. I had just returned the day before from a mission to Treasury with six LCIs. I'm sitting with CDR Smith (our flotilla commander) enjoying Bob Hope and Bing Crosby in an old picture, when the orderly comes to CDR Smith with a dispatch. He puts a flashlight on it, reads it, and hands it to me. "Here's a job for you. Bring six LCIs to Bougainville." I read it. Six LCIs were wanted to pick up a battalion of

Marine paratroopers at Vella Lavella and join a Task Force proceeding to Bougainville.

After the movie, Jannotta went to Commander Smith's headquarters hut to check over the ships available. They selected six whose turn it was to go (including Jannotta's flagship). Back in his cabin Jannotta planned the mission and sent a message to the commanding officers of the six ships to report to him at once. When assembled, he gave them typed copies of the movement order and briefed them verbally on course, speed and time schedule, cruising formation, codes and signals to be used for communication, loading and unloading troops and equipment methods, and attack doctrine—that is, what they were to do in the event of submarine or air attack while they are underway or at Bougainville.

The next morning at 0745 Jannotta went to the bridge, sent up a flag hoist to get underway in a single column at a distance of 200 yards. At 0800 his group joined up with two destroyers which would act as escorts. He informed the destroyers that he would navigate for the Task Unit. He then set course and speeds to reach Vella Lavella at 0530, November 22, and requested the destroyers take station for screening. He spent the night on the bridge or in the chart house, checking track, speed and position of the unit, and the following of the other ships in course changes. There were occasional rain squalls, but the visibility was good, and the sea was moderate. The moon was no longer full which made them less vulnerable to night plane attacks. However, at 0310 they heard a plane overhead, a snooper. "At night, in company with other ships," Jannotta noted, "we don't fire on it. No ship fires unless it is directly attacked because if it is a single plane on patrol, it cannot do too much damage, and to fire would disclose position and strength of the Task Unit." This aircraft was alone—it circled for half an hour, then two bombs exploded to the right and astern of the last ship in one column, and left. No shots fired—no ship damage or personnel casualties. He continued:

At 0526 we were opposite our landing beach (at Vella Lavella) about 1/2 mile out as it was just beginning to

83

get light. At 0531 my ship hit the beach and the other 5 followed successfully on my left flank, about 15 yards apart (the beach area here was very narrow). The destroyer stood off about a mile, cruising back and forth, on guard. All ships at battle stations.

The paratroopers were all set for us on the beach—lined up by company, each man carrying his own pack and weapons, and each company's supplies (rations, water, ammunition, etc., about 20 tons per company) piled separately, ready to load, one company per ship. I contacted the battalion commander. Each ship contacted the company commanders to instruct them on loading, which was done smoothly and efficiently in about 45 minutes. This was a tough and well-trained outfit, LCOL Krulak's 2nd Marine Parachute Battalion, the same bunch we had pulled out of Choiseul about three weeks ago when they were practically surrounded by Japs. We had plenty of air coverage over us—our own fighters—and no Jap planes came in. It was with considerable relief, though, that I was able to signal ships to retract—my own last, since, when we're lined up on the beach, loading or unloading, as close together as that morning, we make a good target.

By 0700 all ships were off the beach, in formation, the destroyers screening ahead; then, we were on our way, making 14 knots now because we had to rendezvous about 60 miles out with the ships of another task group.

Upon joining the task group, I was no longer responsible for the navigation and time schedule for the ships—the OTC (officer in tactical command) was a four-striper (captain) on one of the destroyers. I stayed on the bridge during the night. Ships were darkened, visibility closed down (no moon until about 0300 in the morning). Gradually, groups of troops, talking or singing on deck, broke up and turned in to their bunks in the troop compartments. With the naked eye you could see the ship ahead, astern and to the side; the phosphorescent waves out of the dark mass of most of the other ships and of the destroyers screening the flanks—not those ahead. When the moon came up visibility was considerably better—though, thank goodness, it was not the period of full moon. Nights like these you feel the curious combination and quiet, stealth, alertness, and expectancy of ships and men at sea on a war mission.

At 0435, about an hour out from Bougainville, we heard planes overhead and went to battle stations. For some time nothing happened—we could see nothing—just hear the hum of plane motors, now loud, now fading out as they flew around. Suddenly they started dropping flares over us and the whole area seemed almost as light as day—the ships all around standing out sharp and distinct. It gave you a feeling of positive nudity. The formation kept moving on—waiting for the attack, which seemed an almost interminable time in coming. Pretty soon, and just as the last of the flares were fading out, streams of tracer-lighted 20mms and single bursts of 40mms streaked up from ships ahead and to starboard.

By this time we were only two or three miles from shore, and the dark outline of Bougainville's mountains showed indistinctly. Then shore batteries started firing, and shore searchlights fingered out into the sky. They got one plane in the light—a tiny, silvery gleaming dot, and the shots burst all around it as it turned and dove out of the lights. The attack was centered on the foremost ships in the formation and along the shore for which we were headed. I don't know how many planes there were, but there must have been quite a number because they dropped a powerful lot of bombs for a period of 10 minutes or more—geysers of water leaping up around the ships, and blooms of white smoke blossoming along the shore. We saw one plane hit and streak down in flame—and were told two others were also shot down. We were carrying our horseshoes in the right place—because not a single ship was hit, nor did the task group have any casualties. They did much damage on shore, though (around Navy headquarters), as I found when I got ashore later. The firing stopped just as suddenly as it had started—and we heard no more planes. A few minutes later it started to lighten up, and I put on speed pulling the other LCIs with me to pass through and ahead of the formation for the beach.

The beach is a beauty—sandy, sharply shelving—and much of it—and while there are quite a number of reefs and shoals in front of it, we knew where they were and hit the beach in perfect order—my ship on the left flank, the other ships successively to my right—about 50 yards apart. Ramps were down and troops disembarking in a few seconds. Within 20 minutes the last case of ammunition, etc., was off and we were starting to retract. We were in, unloaded, and on the way out to sea before the first LST was anywhere near its beach. Since the Admiral insists all ships be escorted, I now lay in wait around 9 or 10 hours while the LSTs and supply ships were unloaded, and the entire Task Group was ready to form up and start back. So I instructed the LCIs to keep under way within an area one half to one mile from shore, in event of air attack, and signaled for a boat to take me ashore. I wanted to try again to contact Nick, and I had to report to Navy headquarters to arrange for loading any casualties to be returned to Guadalcanal.

When I went ashore, I found the area around the beach and headquarters somewhat messed up from the bombing in the early morning as we were coming in, and from shells the Japs had lobbed in the afternoon before. When I tried to use the phone to locate Nick's outfit, I had no luck—the telephone lines had been blown out here and there and it would be several hours before I could get through to him; his outfit was some distance away by Jeep, and I couldn't be away from my ships long enough to try to get there and back, so I had to be content with leaving a note for him which headquarters promised to deliver, and a message which they promised to phone as soon as the lines were fixed up. I had also given the major in command of the paratroopers we brought in a note to deliver to Nick—he knew Nick's outfit and colonel well. So Nick will hear from me, but I was badly disappointed I couldn't see or talk to him.

They had about 230 casualties (ambulatory cases—not litter cases, which are evacuated by LSTs) they wanted me to evacuate to Guadalcanal on LCIs, so I arranged time and place for beaching two LCIs to take them on.

Had breakfast with Captain Oliver O. Kessing, Naval Commander ashore, whom I had met in Noumea—and was about ready to leave for my ship when the air raid alarm started howling and everyone started diving for foxholes. Captain Kessing invited me in his—quite a good one, but I declined with thanks and said I'd accept a boat that would get me out to my ship, instead. I've been caught ashore during air raids before—at Rendova—and I don't like any part of the business of diving into a wet, dirty foxhole or in the mud under a truck.

Well, I started out in a Higgins boat (amphibious landing craft) and I couldn't see my ship (the 328) which I had ordered to stand off about one-quarter mile out and keep a lookout for me. Then I realized I had told them to get going (full speed) and keep going during an air attack—and they sure as hell had. They were at least two miles away from me—and had forgotten all about me. I chased them around for 45 minutes before I finally caught up with them, and was fit to be tied.

This attack was by a small force of bombers—we didn't see more than 10 to 12—with a number of Zeros—and they never got in on the ships or the shore forces. We had a flock of fast, hard-hitting P38s giving us air coverage, and they drove them off. I took my ship and another into a different beach to load on the wounded. Gunshot, shrapnel, bomb, and shell splinter cases, for the most part, don't seem as bad or as pitiful to me as the shell shock, had "war neurosis" cases. We had quite a number of these aboard—

coherent thought, emotional control knocked completely out of them—they have to be led around and watched—they fall in a heap or jump into the air or just sit all day, dumb and shivering, every time a gun goes off or a bomb or shell explodes. Most of them will get over it—but it's a long, slow pull back to normalcy for those lads.

The Japs had finally lugged some batteries of mortars over the mountains (from Buin) and were shelling some of our positions. Our own artillery was popping off periodically. One of the areas the Japs had under fire was the beaching area—but my LCIs had gone in and out before they opened up. Now they were shelling pretty regularly and shells were beginning to land 100 to 150 yards from us. So I pushed the loading of the casualties as much as I could and finally got both ships off the beach and headed out to sea. While we were still only 300 to 400 yards off the beach, one Jap battery finally got the range on the LSTs that had been unloading next to us. At least half a dozen shells landed smack on two of them. We heard them over the radio calling the destroyers—giving the approximate location of the battery—and asking for fire support. One of them came rushing in from the patrol—steamed in to within 500 yards of the shore about one-half mile down the coast, and started firing everything it had around the position of the Jap battery. They really poured it in for about 20 minutes. There was no more shelling from that vicinity for the rest of the day. The LSTs had no serious ship damage—but lost 18 men. The dead were buried ashore—not far from the beach—within an hour.

About 1300, I was advised by the OTC that the task group would form and get under way at 1700. At 1345 I began to get reports over the radio (from air fighter control) of bogeys headed our way. "Bogeys" is the term used for unknown or enemy plane formation. For about half an hour we charted the reported positions—and now we were getting reports on three (one a large formation of 35 planes; two of

The invasion at Empress Augusta Bay gets under way on Bougainville,
November 1943. *AP Photo*

15 to 20 each) coming from different directions. I flashed the "Enemy planes—take battle stations" to all my ships— the destroyers did likewise. All ships speeded up—LCIs had destroyers—started zigzagging, and working in nearer to shore to give the LSTs still on the beaches support. Our P38s, about 12 of them, started taking altitude, patrolling in pairs and fours. Pretty soon we sighted the first lot— flying high and headed our way—counted 19 of them. They started bombing over the ships as they came in. One destroyer, about a mile out, was blanked out in a complete pattern of water geysers all around it, but was not hit, and that was the closest any of that bunch came to any ships. We had about four land among the LCIs but at least 300 or 400 yards away. Only the destroyers were firing—they were too high up for our guns. Within a couple of minutes our fighters were into them, and turned them away. They got one, before we lost sight of them. But in the meantime another group suddenly appeared from nowhere and started diving at individual ships. Two of them, flying almost wing to wing, decided to take one of the LCIs—and while I stood there on the bridge, holding my breath and expecting it to blow it to little pieces, they didn't bomb—they strafed, from stern to stern, and were in and out and away in nothing flat (most likely these Japanese planes had already expended their ordnance and the only weapons available were their machine guns).

Although at least three of our ships were within range and got in several bursts and a number of shells were seen to hit, we didn't knock either of them down. As far as I know, none of this bunch were shot down, but also, as far as I know, they didn't come close to any other ship—the A.A. fire from all ships, which was a truly formidable screen, held them off. I signaled the LCI that had been directly attacked for a damage report and wasn't reassured any when I got a "will report shortly". When I did get the report it was worse than I expected—11 casualties—mostly among their gun crews, which was the reason they hadn't been able to return fire more effectively. They had been strafed—not with machine gun bullets, but with 20mm shells. None killed, by a miracle of good fortune, but 6 of the 11 seriously wounded and requiring immediate hospitalization. I sent the LCI alongside an LST, which carries our doctors and surgeons and is equipped with operating rooms, etc., for transfer of these six. I went aboard, and found young Cobb (the CO) had everything shipshape and under perfect control, talked with the men and found that their morale was truly wonderful. One youngster—Cobb said he's 19—a gunner's mate—with a good sized shell fragment through the upper part of this right leg, and a nasty hole in his right side, grinned up at me and said, "They sure raised hell with us this time, sir, but it'll be our turn next."

The last ship was finally unloaded shortly after 1700 and standing out to sea. The LSTs formed up in two columns. I brought my LCIs in position astern of them—the destroyers gathered from all directions and took screening positions ahead and on the flanks—and we were headed back. The OTC signaled the course changes for the night and ordered all ships to fly their ensigns at half mast from 0800 until sunset the following day in memory of the men of the task group who had been killed this day.

We had a quiet night and an uneventful day, except for the burial at sea of another of the LST men hit yesterday. We should arrive off Guadalcanal about 0830 in the morning, where we'll unload our casualties to trucks that should be waiting for them. The task group will then be dissolved, and I'll take my LCIs across to Florida Island to our anchorage and beaching area in Hutchinson Point.

Tomorrow is Thanksgiving. All ships have had turkey issued to them—we got ours before we left this trip. The men are looking forward to it.

Darling, when I started this letter (hours ago—it's now very, very late) I had no intention of getting off on this long story and writing such a book. I seem to have been in the mood to unburden a bit. I hope it won't burden you. And if I've talked much about myself you, I know, will understand and not put me down as a rank braggart or super-egotist.

The censor, I hope, will appreciate the fact that there is no information here that the Jap doesn't already have, or if he doesn't have, would do him any good. Nor is there information that our American people haven't already been given—by press, radio or official pronouncement.

I'll be thinking of you, my darling, this Thanksgiving Day—and of our girls—Nick and grandson. We'll have a true Thanksgiving when we're all together again. What a celebration that will be!!!! Worlds of love to Mary Fran and to you, my beloved.

Vernon

—————

USS LCI L 328
November 28, Florida Island, Solomons

My Darling,

Hope you have received some of my letters by now. I am well, but boy, is it hot—during the day we practically bathe in perspiration. The nights are cool, though. Rain hasn't started yet—that is, no more than the usual showers several times a day. The rainy season they say is really something, though—then it really rains. I miss you, Sweetheart, and I love you with all my heart. It won't be long until Christmas now. I received two packages (Xmas) from you, I think, yesterday, but I won't open them until then. All the other men are doing the same thing—saving the opening of their packages until Xmas. This will be our first Christmas apart, darling, out of 26 since we were married. Even in the last war, I got home just in time for our first Christmas together—remember? No such luck this time. Four more of our skippers, though (including two from my group—Townsend and Therkield) are being returned this next month (December) to the States, for new ships. They'll be flown back, and should be home for Xmas. That's quite a break, isn't it? There isn't a thing I can send you, or Mary Fran, or Diane, or Shirley, or Nicky for Christmas. You'll understand, I know. But I'll be thinking of you—and about what a swell one we'll have together next year. I hope you'll have a gay time at Christmas. If we're in port, we're going to have a party at the Officers' Club at Lynns Point. I'll drink a toast to you, my darlings.

All my love,
Vernon

PACIFIC WAR STRATEGY

To protect the northern flank of the successful Allied landings in the Solomon Islands, Admiral Nimitz received approval in May 1943 to initiate a second offensive front across the Central Pacific Islands. From east to west they included the Gilberts, Marshalls, Carolines, Marianas, and Palau. To open the new front, a 5th Fleet was formed under Vice Admiral Spruance. First stop: Tarawa, November 22-23, 1943. It required attacking a well-defended atoll, but despite three days of horrific fighting and 3,400 casualties the Marines prevailed. The tactical and logistical lessons learned in assaulting the armed beaches at Tarawa would benefit the Allies at "places like Normandy, Luzon, Iwo Jima, and Okinawa". Tarawa was followed by landings at Kwajalein and Eniwetok (Marshalls), and Saipan, Guam and Tinian (Marianas).

When Admiral Spruance put Marines ashore at Saipan on June 15, 1944, the newly designated 1st Mobile Fleet under Vice Admiral Jisaburō Ozawa had already sortied out of Tawi Tawi, in the Sulu Archipelago (an island between Mindanao and Borneo) with the intent to destroy the US 5th fleet "with one blow". It was a sizable enemy force of 5 carriers, 4 light carriers, 5 battleships, 11 heavy cruisers, 2 light cruisers, and 28 destroyers. The Japanese faced Admiral Spruance's 5th Fleet, which consisted of 7 carriers, 8 light carriers, 7 battleships, 8 heavy cruisers, 13 light cruisers, and 69 destroyers. The disparity in forces was even more obvious in combat carrier aircraft: the Japanese had 430 carrier aircraft to put in the air against 891 US carrier aircraft. More important, though, the American pilots were combat-tested and highly trained; typically junior pilots had 18 to 24 months' training and 300 hours' flying before joining the fleet, whereas most Japanese pilots were green with less than six months of training. On June 17, as Ozawa's forces converged on Saipan, Spruance elected to keep his carriers in a defensive mode rather than attack the 1st Mobile Fleet, fearing an end run by Japanese forces that would leave US Amphibious Operations vulnerable. On the 19th, Ozawa attacked in four waves; from the first one of 68 planes, 41 were shot down by F6F Hellcats. In the second wave of 109, 97 were scratched by Hellcats. In the third raid of 47, 7 aircraft were shot down, and only a few of the attackers made it through to the US fleet, causing minimal damage. The fourth raid, because of faulty navigation, broke into two groups and lost 66 aircraft—one segment was jumped by F6Fs while in a landing pattern at Guam and lost 49 aircraft. The results prompted an American pilot to comment, "Hell, this is like an old time turkey shoot." From then on, pilots referred to it as the "great Marianas turkey shoot."

At the time, Admiral Spruance was criticized by many US Naval officers for remaining at the beaches and not aggressively pursuing the Japanese fleet. However, in retrospect, a total of approximately 600 Japanese aircraft, both carrier- and land-based, were lost. In the end, the Battle of the Philippine Sea effectively neutralized the Imperial Japanese Navy's air offensive capability. During the fighting, US lost 123 aircraft, primarily due to emergency night carrier landings.

Eighth Fleet Headquarters. Kawanishi is in the back row,
third from left, Buin, Bougainville Island.

Chapter XI
THE NEW MISSION GETS UNDER WAY

IMPERIAL JAPANESE NAVAL BASE
BUIN, BOUGAINVILLE ISLAND
NOVEMBER 18, 1943

When the Allies bypassed Buin and landed at Empress Bay, far up the Bougainville coast, Kawanishi received a new assignment that must have filled him with pride. He would take charge of the supply effort at Buka Island, just across a small channel from Bougainville's northern tip. From there, the commanders told him, the job was to direct logistics for supplying the troops now battling the Americans at Empress Augusta Bay.

But some days after receiving the new assignment, he was pulled in and given the additional job of leading a march through the little-known terrain of Bougainville's interior. The assignment was all part of the new supply program, they explained; the trek north was part of an effort to move the majority of the 3,000 non-fighting labor and construction personnel from Buin to Buka Island and eventually all the way to Rabaul. Removing these construction workers was essential to streamlining the supply effort because they would not be consuming precious food needed to keep real soldiers fit for battle.

He received his challenging orders stoically. For a young officer, it was nearly all he could do to keep his emotions from settling into his face and demeanor. Here they were telling him he would lead almost 300 men on a journey through jungles and over mountain passes.

The 300 men at his command were not soldiers. They were laborers; provincials from Japan or even the more-disdained Koreans who were seen as second-class slave laborers. In the hierarchy of the Japanese military and even larger society, these men were not seen as valuable in themselves. This dynamic created a tension for Kawanishi who, regardless, saw them as human beings, yet was conflicted by a societal feeling of separation from them.

The treatment of Korean workers was one of many questions on his mind; mostly, the fact that he was a junior officer with a lot of experience at mundane paper-shuffling duties, but with none at directing troops in the field. He had never been tested in battle. But a chilling uncertainty in the faces of his superiors told him they knew these things all too well.

In the quiet of night, as he lay in his bunk, this new turn of events left Kawanishi feeling the burden of responsibility, the drag of the potential to blemish his as yet untarnished reputation among his fellow junior officers. He would be in charge of these men, and their safety and well-being would be dependent on him and him alone. But his pride chased away his negative thoughts. He was used to the slightly sour taste of this blend of emotions, ones that had come from his role as oldest male in the family.

For now there was nothing to do but plan as carefully as he could, using maps that contained absolutely no information on large swaths of the countryside. If there were more time—he had less than two weeks to plan and supply his mission—Kawanishi would have liked to give proper attention to saying goodbye to his friends on the Buin staff who were to remain at the front. They also faced an uncertain future.

Kawanishi spent hours trying to get on top of the mission his commanders had assigned him. His eyes kept returning to the troubling empty spots on his hand-drawn maps. These blank, uncharted places left him feeling slightly hopeless. To make matters worse, each time he questioned soldiers who'd ventured beyond the immediate surroundings of Buin, their responses left him no better informed.

When the time came, Kawanishi packed minimally, discarding a host of extra clothes and other odds and ends. But carefully tucked into his rucksack lay his journal and an assortment of pencils.

November 30, 1943

At 0800, we assembled in the jungle at supply headquarters. We were set to move out at 1000. I walked through where the laborers had been assembled. They looked like a band of downtrodden beggars, drifters. Still, their morale was high. After all, they were leaving Buin, which was being bombed daily, to go to Buka and then by ship to Rabaul. Just as I was thinking I would go bid farewell to Captain Ikeda, the high whine of the air raid sirens began. Air raids over the last two or three days had targeted the airfield, and I didn't pay much attention to the sirens until a bomb exploded right over my head, followed by a horrific roar. I ran out of the barracks and looked up to see a B-25 flying through a gap in the jungle so low that I thought I could touch it. That instant an explosion and a blast of wind and noise hurled me to the ground with such force that it seemed to split my head wide open. When I attempted to stand up, another explosion knocked me senseless. The air was filled with the roar of explosions and the trees shook violently. I realized this was a major air raid. As I ran into an air raid shelter, a third bomb exploded.

The shelter was jammed with workers lying prone in the dirt, their hands covering their ears. Words cannot describe what I felt as the explosions steadily approached where we were. I felt helplessness, and terror welled up from the pit of my stomach and overwhelmed me. I tried to hide the terror I felt by shouting, "That was a close one!" But just at that instant, a head-crushing blast seemed to rip the shelter apart, completely wiping away the calm façade I was trying to put on.

After a few seconds, I came to my senses and lifted my head. I had been lying right on top of the sweat-drenched body of a laborer. Dirt was trickling slowly down from the ceiling. I tried to sound nonchalant when I gave the all clear, but the words came out weak and hoarse. The roar of the squadron, bombs dropping randomly, the explosions, the vibrations—it all had pushed me to the brink of madness and had filled me with an awful physically crushing despair. It took all my effort to keep from screaming. And yet the shelter was as silent as a morgue. The laborers just lay where they were, flat on the ground in the dark.

How many minutes had it lasted? I bolted out of the pitch-black shelter only to be momentarily stunned by the blinding sunlight. This dark and covered corner of the jungle was now laid completely bare to the searing tropical sunlight of high noon. The shattered remains of the barracks and uprooted trees were strewn everywhere. Looking up, I saw what few trees remained, their barren branches reaching forlornly into the cloudless sky.

The air was filled with the mingling odor of burnt sulfur and tree sap. This peculiarly acidic and sharp smell wafted through the air and seeped into the deepest recesses of my brain—a smell I'm sure I'll never forget. Around my feet, leaves pulverized into tiny shards rustled dryly in the light breeze. The whole place was utterly silent, as if that terrible, horrific bombardment had never happened at all. My exhaustion overwhelmed me. I quietly closed my eyes. I felt the pain of the blazing sun on my skin. At some point, I drifted off into my own inner world.

I heard shouts and opened my eyes. I realized I had to snap out of my torpor. I walked a few steps and then realized for the first time what had happened. Amid the churn of foliage, I hadn't noticed, but the gaping mouth of a 10-meter crater left by a 250-kilogram bomb was just a few meters away. Great heaps of earth covered in ashen leaves encircled the crater. Our barrack had been reduced to nothing but a wreck of scattered lumber.

One of the air raid shelters had collapsed from a direct hit. Two men ran out from a remaining exit, screaming that they'd been hit. Their faces were black with gunpowder. They bled badly. I ordered some soldiers to *dig out the shelter, and out came body after body. Shovels digging into the dirt struck dismembered arms. We used boards as pallets to carry away bodies. I went about this in a daze. I knew we had to hurry up and get going, but my mind reeled at the thought of moving out.*

An hour later, I had everyone lined up in the area cleared by the bombing. The night before I had imagined that the moment of departure would be deeply emotional for me. Now the moment had actually arrived and I didn't feel anything. Rather than emotion, I felt nothing more than an instinctive urge to get out of there as fast as possible, and a raw fatigue from the stress brought on by the heavy responsibility placed upon me.

After bidding an official farewell to Captain Ikeda, everyone got into the trucks that had been sent to transport us the 12 kilometers the road lasted. I gave the order to move out, and the trucks lurched slowly forward. On the way, I bid farewell to the Chief of Eighth Fleet Headquarters. Our long journey had begun at last.

After crossing a low-hanging bridge over the River Muriko, the road got really bad, and we halted our truck and waited for the other two trucks that had fallen behind—I ordered someone to go check on them and then sat down on the grass.

Meanwhile, the laborers had formed into little groups of three, four and five, and their banter was making something of a commotion. Their world seemed completely different from mine—they were almost like wild animals, completely without decorum. I decided to put a stop to their unruly behavior. I tried talking to a few of them but I wasn't getting through at all.

One of the laborers was already eating some of his dried bread. Our food had to hold us a week, all the way until the next supply point, and carelessly eating even a single piece of bread now might mean starvation in the jungle later on. We had to conserve our food like a desert

*traveler has to conserve water. In my sternest voice, I told
this worker to stop eating at once. But he was from the
countryside and didn't really understand what I was saying, though he seemed to have a vague sense he was being
dressed down. When I finished talking, he went right back
to eating.*

*I called Warrant Officer Uchida over. A 40-year-
old noncommissioned officer who'd been in the military
quite a while, Uchida was a fearless character in charge
of the laborers in the supply section. A boat captain before
entering the navy, he was an intelligent man who had seen
more than his share of troubles in a changing world. And
he had a reputation as the man most capable at handling
these laborers.*

*I ordered him to get the workers to stop eating up
all their bread. With a glint in his eyes, he saluted and
got down to business. "Anyone eating bread, stand up!"
he shouted as he walked about scowling at the groups of
laborers. A few men rose warily, like frogs being sized up
by a snake. He gathered all the bread offenders together
and said sternly, "When you're told don't grub, don't grub!"
Then he kicked a few of them for good measure. That ended
the whole problem right then and there.*

*The whole scene left me with a sense of powerlessness.
I felt completely isolated and apart from these men. I
despaired at the thought of leading them through all of the
troubles that undoubtedly lay ahead. How could a young
man like me take command of this disorderly bunch? And
to make matters worse, the order to march had been made
so hastily that none of my most trusted subordinates could
come. But the bread incident turned out to have a silver
lining. After that, Warrant Officer Uchida took care of all
sorts of little details for me and proved indispensable to me
during the trek.*

*It gradually grew dark. A white fog formed and
drifted slowly over the river. Sundown came at 1600 on*

Bougainville, which lay far to the east end of the time zone in the Southern Hemisphere. When the sun settled behind the mountains, the whole place fell silent and grew dark. I really wanted to reach the place I had marked on our map as our first day's destination, but the other trucks still hadn't caught up. I grew depressed at the thought of having to change our schedule on the very first day of our journey.

Still, I decided I had no choice but to give the order to halt and prepare dinner. All the laborers happily went down to the river's edge to begin making dinner. A tin can dangling from each of their waists was the only eating utensil they possessed. The white smoke of numerous little campfires soon appeared and drifted upward. I suddenly became terribly disconsolate. My role as an officer in the military, the responsibility I was presumed to be worthy of—these things were just a sham. I watched the darkness descend over the river and the white smoke of the campfires. I felt so helpless and weak I wanted to cry.

I lay down on the grass and looked up at the slowly changing sky. Finally, the other trucks came lumbering slowly over the bridge. Relieved, I stood up. Ensign Takahashi came and reported in his bold voice that one of the trucks had broken down. His polished, forthright manner somehow lifted my spirits.

Finally, the whole group of 270 was together and dinner began. I joined a group of laborers and, under flashlight, began a dinner of rice and beef rations.

After dinner, I discussed our situation with Ensign Takahashi. We decided to stick to our original plan and go as far as the foot of Mount Hachiman that evening. We departed at 1800 on foot, the trucks having gone back. The road was three meters wide but in terrible condition— nothing more than 50-cm deep, water-filled tire tracks. We had a few flashlights to light the way, but not nearly enough for such a large group on such a treacherous road.

We worked our way over the muddy quagmire in silence. We took a short break every 30 minutes. The evening breeze felt good on our sweat-drenched bodies. The road got gradually steeper, and we had to lift our knees straight up to make any progress. After two hours of this, we were exhausted. We caught sight of two little army patrol shacks on the side of the road. Interior light shone occasionally between blue mosquito nets fluttering in the breeze. I felt a brief pang of homesickness at seeing this. We were a sorry sight, covered in mud, working our way down this road in the dark. A distant light in the night will always make the wanderer yearn for the warmth of home.

We couldn't find a good campsite, so we finally set up on the side of the road. I took off my gaiters and stretched my legs. I changed my sweat-soaked shirt. I took off the shirt I wore to ward off the heat and changed into fatigues. It felt so good to change into dry clothes. The day's trek was over. I thought about everything that had happened that day and fell asleep.

December 1, 1943

We woke up at 0400. Dawn comes early in the South Pacific, and it was already getting light. We woke the laborers, who were covered in mud and sleeping scattered about like old rags, and ordered them to get ready to move out. Gradually the camp came to life. I changed back into my sweaty shirt and tropical weather fatigues from the day before. Their clammy coldness made me shiver. A fine mist gently floated over the tarp. I tied a rope around my fatigues. Once I had put on my sword and attached my rubber map pouch, canteen, duffle bag, and cloth with an elastic band, I was ready to go. I gathered up my dry clothes and rain parka and put them in my duffle bag.

I stretched my stiff legs.

Since we wanted to make Hachiman Mountain before the day's air raids began, we decided to march first and eat breakfast later. We started off in the morning chill with the haste of a column under enemy pursuit. It was just the second day, and everyone's legs were still strong. I took the lead, Ensign Takahashi the rear, and Warrant Officer Uchida and another named Yamamoto took charge of the middle of the column.

At 0600, we arrived at a cluster of huts at the foot of Hachiman Mountain. We could see trails of white campfire smoke, and birdsong filled the air. The huts—accommodations for about 30 men stationed there by the army—were scattered about the area. Seeing these dwellings during the course of our march made me truly homesick. This cleared, pristine space under jungle trees had the ambience of people going about normal daily life. For people who have only experienced life in civilized surroundings, it might be hard to imagine, but I felt real joy when we came to spots like these in the middle of the jungle transformed by human hands.

We stopped for breakfast. The leftover rice from the night before tasted delicious. We rinsed our mouths in the cold, invigorating water of a stream running alongside us. The place had the charm of a mountain valley back home. I stretched out on a log. Birdsong roused pleasant emotions within me. It was heartwarming to watch the laborers go about this and that in their usual ramshackle, haphazard way, and I felt the beginning of a feeling of real affection for them.

We resumed marching at 0800. We eventually made it to the base of the Hachiman range, a peak dubbed Santarō. Once we crossed this peak, we would be well on the way to the eastern coastline. We had heard nothing but how hard this part of the trek would be, and the whole column was a picture of abject misery as I led them up the pass. The pass had both an old road and a newer one. We elected to take the somewhat longer new road because we heard it would be easier going. There wasn't a cloud in the sky. Though it was still early, the scorching sun was already slowing down our pace. Wiping away sweat was a waste of effort, and its salty residue gradually turned the skin a whitish hue. We wound our way up the steep mountainside on the meter-wide road. The jagged rocks made the going even more difficult. The road left the dense jungle that enveloped it, and we entered a valley that felt like walking into a sauna. The intense heat and humidity was enough to drive you mad. Ferns, wisteria, and hemp palm formed walls of vegetation, their fallen leaves covering the ground more than 30 centimeters deep. We had walked into a twilight world in which our footsteps were the only sound. We struggled forward. We finally topped the ridge and felt reborn by the tepid breeze that met us there. It wasn't much of a breeze, but it was enough for us all to let loose a cheer and breathe a sigh of relief.

After five hours of merciless marching, we had finally reached the top of the mountain. We took a short rest. Through the trees to the south, we could see the Buin plain. A few steps further and the eastern coastal mountains came into view right before us. I sat down on a rock and wiped away my sweat. I savored the southwest breeze blowing through the mountains and thought about my life back in Buin.

A stream of memories came forth of what had been a truly pleasant life among good friends. And now the bonds formed over a year of work, bonds of real affection were being completely ripped away. Who among us would be the first to die I had no way of knowing, but it seemed more than likely we'd never meet again. The fate of the 270 exhausted men resting around me was now entirely in my hands. I was to confront my fate alone. It really brought home what a truly strange thing fate is. I stood up on the tips

of my feet to get another look at Buin from where we were,
but it had vanished under the mists.

I gobbled down my lunch, completely lost in thought.
Suddenly, the clouds started to roil. A harsh, cold wind
blew from the south. The entire Buin plain had now
disappeared in a shroud of clouds, and a fine misty rain
began to fall. As it rained, I bid my final farewell to Buin.
In the misty rain, a white parrot flew across the valley:

A parrot, flying
I am struck by its color
Crossing the valley,
A light rain is drizzling
Across Mount Santarō.

US soldiers on Bougainville, Solomon Islands, March 1944. *US Army*

Chapter XII
TREKKING UP BOUGAINVILLE
DECEMBER 1943

As Kawanishi began his trek up Bougainville, Jannotta shared a piece of news with his wife.

> About a week ago we got word that Admiral Forte (Commander Landing Craft Flotillas) was going to start sending LCIs to Australia on a recreation cruise—a few at a time. Some excitement: six were to go on the first trip. CDR Smith decided that the fairest way to handle the selection of ships, since all were equally deserving, was to put the ships' numbers in one hat, the flagship numbers in another, the group commanders' names in still another, and draw to see which ships would go, which flagship would be among them and which group commander would take them. Four of the ships in my group and two in CDR Byrd's group were the lucky ones, and CDR Byrd hit the jackpot. He left with them several days ago— they'll be gone about a month— one week each way to make the trip; two weeks at Sydney, which everyone says is the best liberty port in Australia. That has certainly pepped everyone up, and while nothing is certain in the Navy until you have the orders in hand, and events might make it impossible to even send one more group of six, let alone all, still, the presumption is that over that period of the next few months every ship and LCIer will

get a two weeks' liberty in Sydney. One of the beauties of it is that this will not be counted as "leave" against anyone, since the ships are ordered to the port.

I'd like to see Australia myself. I've heard so much about it, and have met a number of fine Australian officers up here. However, I'm not counting on it. I'll believe it, and look forward to it, only when I have orders in my hands, and have set sail with some of our ships.

A LEADER EMERGES
December 1, 1943

As Kawanishi carefully packed his diary with its latest entries, he scanned the landscape surrounding Santarō Pass. Two hundred and seventy men lay about in small groups taking a welcome break from a tough morning climb. It was tempting to continue resting, but if the mist and rain cleared, they would be exposed to enemy aircraft. Just the previous week, soldiers caught in the open at Santarō Pass had been strafed and killed. With that thought, Kawanishi stood, heaved on his rucksack and ordered the men to move out. It would be another grueling day, one that tested his leadership but also called forth empathy for his men.

We started down at 1300. The rain made the red clay of the road gradually more slippery. We had to find our footing with each step. Still, the rain felt good on our hot skin and everyone perked up. Road conditions continued to deteriorate as we wound our way through mountain vegetation. Occasionally, we'd catch a glimpse through a break in the jungle foliage of the rows of lush green mountains ahead of us. Fog rose up from the deep valleys below. Our rucksacks heavy with moisture, our shirts clinging to our bodies, gradually dampened our spirits. Silently, we started to pick up the pace.

Midway, the road joined with the older road and widened. The slope gradually leveled off as well. Here and

110

there, the dense jungle would give way to a stretch that was all Manila hemp and different kinds of ferns, especially at lower altitudes. Muddy water also settled into these low-lying areas to form swamps. There was no place to sit when going through these places. Water worked its way into your boots and tabi (traditional Japanese socks) and then into your tired and swollen feet. All we could do was keep walking.

By the afternoon, we were running late. The plan for the day was to make it down the mountain to the Luluai River. We wanted to get there by 1500 so we could set up camp. I picked up the pace. Walking seven straight hours in the rain had pushed our endurance to the limit. I clenched my teeth from pain and exhaustion. Mere willpower kept my legs moving. I gripped my sword in my right hand and a walking stick in the left. Sometimes I'd turn around, straighten up the column, and exhort everyone to keep up and not straggle behind. The men were in obvious pain, their faces contorted from the extreme discomfort they felt. But the fear of falling behind, of getting lost and dying in the jungle focused them to their task. They bore their pain and trudged forward.

Among the laborers was a man over 50. He had been the captain of a fishing boat that had been requisitioned and pressed into service. But the boat was sunk en route. He has yet to go home, and though he yearns to go back, he has been made a laborer. Sometimes I'd give him words of encouragement and he'd look back at me, his wrinkled face a portrait of both innocence and misery. I knew this man's story, having heard it a few times. He had three children and had been living a quiet life back home. The only thing he looked forward to was going back. I'd looked at him, gasping desperately for breath, and wonder why a man like this should be put through such terrible hardship. It was really an awful fate, but there was nothing one could do.

Once again, we entered the great jungle and the road

111

leveled off. As we rounded the last mountain, the dark gray water of the Luluai River came into view. The sight gave my exhausted body a second wind. I turned around and shouted, "We're almost there!" The younger men immediately livened up and in a rush broke ranks. We followed the riverbank. Rounding a bend, we came upon an army garrison that had been stationed there to defend Luluai village.

We would have liked nothing more than to sleep in their barracks. But the idea of entrusting our care to an unfamiliar army unit made us ill at ease, so we decided to set up camp elsewhere. Anyway, we were the navy, and it would have been embarrassing to appear at their base with this motley bunch of laborers. We had our navy pride after all. During a brief rest, I ordered us to cross the river where we would search for a place to make camp.

All the water that flowed down from Hachiman Mountain collected in the Luluai. It was a major river that flowed through the broad valley toward the eastern shoreline. The Luluai was shallow and flowed over a rock-strewn valley floor about 200 meters wide. Coming out of the jungle into this valley with the wide open sky overhead greatly relieved our tension. Though the sky was overcast and gloomy, it still felt good to be in wide open surroundings. We leisurely crossed a little wooden meter-and-a-half-wide bridge, enjoying the gentle river breeze as we went.

We came to a grove of Manila hemp about 1,000 meters from where we crossed and decided to make camp there. The men halted and collapsed into the grass right in their tracks where there they laid for a time unable to move. I, too, lay down. I let the extreme fatigue overtake me; the grass felt wonderful. I closed my eyes. I thought about the way I had lived until just yesterday and compared it with where I was now. Buin now felt like a place very, very far away. I grew discouraged. Boisterous chatter roused

112

me from my reverie. I joined my spirited troops who had already begun to gather firewood for dinner.

Kawanishi gave orders to the squad leaders to build shelters, prepare dinner, and set up a latrine. As he made an inspection tour, "I got a real lift from the way everyone smiled when they greeted me." Everything was in order so he joined the squad leaders to eat—he hung a flashlight overhead and greedily ate the steaming heap of rice in his tin. Before turning in, despite an aching body and feeling dead tired, he decided to make one more inspection tour.

It was then that I noticed one of the men lying down alone by the side of the road. I woke him and asked what he was doing there. He said the squad leaders wouldn't let him sleep in a hut. He looked terribly weak. I called his squad leader over and asked him to explain. Looking somewhat perplexed, the squad leader threw a contemptuous glance at this pathetic-looking man and let loose a torrent of complaints—he wouldn't work with the others, wouldn't follow orders, and on and on.

They might only be laborers, but these men lived and worked according to the strictest of codes. But it seemed that this man had come to the conclusion that his weak constitution meant that the only way he could survive was to not overwork. His group covered for him while he did his best to look busy—but without doing much actual work. Though shunned from the group, he put up with it, because he knew that at least he would be fed. Underneath his weakness was a kind of brazen insolence that went against the most basic everyday norms. Maybe this is how the physically weak get by, I thought.

As I listened to the squad leader's endless list of complaints, I felt as if I were peering into a dark corner of humanity I had never seen before. I ordered the squad leader to put the man in a hut, which he did reluctantly. The man's self-satisfied grin suggested that he felt everything had gone his way. The whole episode left me feeling terribly sullied.

DECEMBER 2, 1943

At 0600, Kawanishi gave the order to move out. He planned to traverse the Hachiman mountain range between the southern tip of the main range that ran north/south across Bougainville and the lowland between the mountains along the coast. The Luluai River ran off the mountains south through the lowlands to the sea. Their goal was to get off the coastal mountains and then follow the Luluai to the eastern shore to a nearby army base at Koromira Point. Kawanishi estimated the distance at about 28 kilometers.

As the sun gets higher, the humidity and heat of the jungle become unbearable. The sweat pours off the body in buckets. The laborers were feeling the strain and their columns grew disorganized. We marched and marched through an endless wall of jungle foliage. Everyone silently bore their intense discomfort and kept on. After maybe another two hours of this, the jungle suddenly gave way and we stood at another branch of the Luluai. It was about lunchtime. The riverbed glared in the midday sun. We took a short break. Relieved, I looked up at the sky. The laborers clambered over baking stones, scooping up water from the river. Others had collapsed in the grass from exhaustion.

Maybe savage heat and humidity drives people crazy, because by then, we were in a state of frenzied distraction. Sitting, walking, standing still—nothing brought any relief. We knew that taking this momentary pleasure would only intensify our hardship later, but we just couldn't help ourselves. We plunged into the lukewarm river water like madmen.

Twenty minutes later, they set off again.

Deep valleys cut across the coastal mountains forcing us to make our way by climbing up and down peaks and valleys in a seesaw fashion. The stifling humidity from before gave way to the blazing heat of direct sunlight, burning our skin raw. Our canteens were soon empty and the sweat that had been pouring out of us gradually dried up. A couple of men collapsed from sunstroke. Those with weak stamina straggled behind the column.

We picked up the pace with nothing to spur us on but the vain hope that we'd find water in the next valley. We started moving with real urgency. Around noon, we descended into a large valley and heard the sound of water. We all let out a woop—"Water! Water!"—and tumbled down the sharp slope. A cool river breeze caressed our faces. In a daze, I leapt into the river. It felt wonderful. I stuck my head into the flowing water and surprised even myself at the amount of water I was gulping down. Groups of stragglers were now showing up on the ridge, and they too came sliding and tumbling down the instant they saw the water below. That river saved us all.

We ate lunch. We rested for perhaps an hour. I worried over whether we should continue any further today. With the workers so exhausted, it might be overdoing it. On the other hand, our food supply meant we absolutely had to stay on schedule. I called Ensign Takahashi over. He looked incredibly exhausted, but he agreed with me. We would move out at 1330. We began marching once again up and down the steep mountains. The trek had become a race to survive.

After two hours, they crossed the last valley and clawed their way up a path "as jagged as a bolt of lighting, and came to a level summit where we were instantly greeted by a vigorously pulsating sea breeze." At last, they could see the sea. Kawanishi sat down to enjoy the moment as the men caught up to him.

115

We had to get moving. "We're almost there," I said energetically and sprang to my feet. The laborers, too, were visibly more spirited. The path sloped gently downward. The sun was low on the horizon and we made good time.

Not long after we moved out, someone reported that one of the men had collapsed with malaria fever. The strain of the morning's march probably brought it on. I was at a momentary loss as to what to do. I couldn't slow the march, but I couldn't leave a sick man behind either. The path was in the middle of the jungle. I told the stricken man that we'd reach our campsite soon and if he could hang in there until then he could rest for a whole day. I had the other men in his squad carry his baggage, had two of them help him walk, and we continued on. We resumed our march down the mountain, our fallen comrade safely in our care.

The road wound slowly down the mountain until we finally reached level ground. The land at the bottom was swamp; the whole area was covered with water. The road ran through it but had been widened to 10 meters by the tracks of army vehicles, which had also turned it into a muddy morass. Pools of water thick with algae filled the tracks. The only way to avoid stepping into water as we moved forward was by walking on exposed tree roots.

The coast had to be close by, but we just couldn't make ourselves go any farther. We found a small rise and decided to make camp there. It was after 1600 and the jungle was already dark. The workers huddled together in little groups. I walked among them saying, "I asked too much of you all today. We'll rest until noon tomorrow, so take it easy." I asked how their feet were doing. I felt real affection for them. I waited into the night for the sick man and his comrades to arrive. The warm reddish glow of campfires appeared.

Like the day before, I changed into dry clothes. I inspected the men's huts, disbursing Atabine (an anti-malarial drug) as I made my rounds. These men had been *given a miserly ration of 15 quinine tablets for the march. It was then that I came to the realization that they were being terribly abused, sent away simply to save rations back at Buin. I felt both pity and love for these men, men who had been cast out like dogs, and a seething resentment toward the people who had forced this disgraceful march upon them. I swore right then and there that I would use every ounce of my strength to protect and defend them.*

Admiral William F. Halsey Jr., seated in center, at a planning session behind the front line on Bougainville, November 1943. *US Navy*

Chapter XIII

HOMESICK

By late November 1943, the Americans had invaded so many islands, large and small, that Jannotta's flotillas had turned their Solomons landings into an art form. These actions demonstrated the Allied Forces' control of the sea and air in the Solomons which, in turn, insured the success of the leapfrogging campaign.

Jannotta, in a November 24, 1943 letter, described the complications of the Solomon offensive. He wrote:

> Of course, out here, the terrific distances involved make the problem of logistics (supply—ammunition, food, equipment, etc.) a very tough one, and it takes time to assemble forces, ships, men, and supplies after one objective is taken for the push on to the next. However, since July 1, our forces (we are a part of the 3rd Amphibious Force, which is a part of the South Pacific Forces under Admiral Halsey) have captured and occupied Rendova, (Munda) New Georgia, Kolombangara, and Vella Lavella (July 1 to October 1), and are now on the job of finishing off the last (to the north) of the Solomons Group.
>
> Our part of the job—that is, the LCI Ls'—is of course transporting combat units from the forward area to assaults, and then the bringing in of reinforcements. Our ships are assigned to various missions 2 to 8 or 10 at a time. So we rotate the mission assignments among all 26 ships in

the flotilla so as to give them all an even break. Then, we rotate the command of these units on missions between the flotilla commander and the three group commanders.

Two days before yesterday, eight new LCI Ls arrived from the States, assigned to our flotilla. Four more are on the way, to make a total of 38—30 troop carriers, 8 gunboat type. The new ones are a decided improvement over the original ones—heavier fire power, more space and changes and additions that our experience over the past 14 months has shown are worthwhile. They seem so spacious and comfortable to us, after the rugged living we've had on the original ones, that we have termed them the "Queen Marys" and the "Gunboats". CDR Smith thinks we ought to shift our flags to the Queen Mary types, pick four new flagships from among these—one for the flotilla commander, and one each for commander groups 13, 14 and 15. I'm not so sure I want to do that, even though the quarters, the equipment, the food, would be much better. I've become attached to the old LCI L 328—I know and can depend on every officer and man—we've been through many tight places together. However, the commander of the flotilla will make the decision—not I.

He continued:

Your letter was certainly well-timed, as tomorrow is my birthday. I think of it only because you and our girls have always made so much of it and been so sweet about it. I miss you constantly, darling, but I'll miss you more tomorrow, and the next tomorrow, until I get home.

During the fall and December of 1943, about half of Jannotta's key commissioned and senior non-commissioned officers were sent back to outfit new ships; in essence, it represented a logical method of expanding the fleet's capability to meet 1944 offensive operations in places like Normandy, France, the Gilberts, the Marshalls, and

Philippine Islands. Nonetheless, training replacements put additional burden on commanding officers like Jannotta.

> Sending four more of my COs back to the States this month to man new ships—Townsend, Therkield, Maxie, McCoy—all fine men who have done a good job. Well, some day I may get a break and get home, too.
>
> I'm leaving on another mission in the morning—nothing important this time. I think most of our action is over now for a little while again, until we are ready for the next jump.
>
> My love to all three of you—worlds and worlds of love. Goodnight, my Sweetheart.

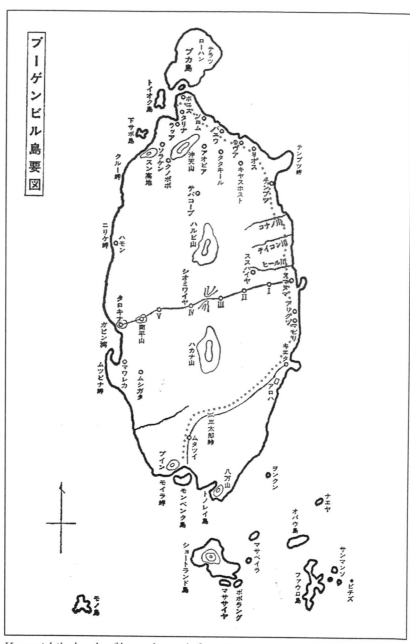

Kawanishi's sketch of his trek north from Buin, Bougainville Island to Buka Island, *Records of Wars on Bougainville Island by an Imperial Japanese Officer*, Kotarō Kawanishi

Chapter XIV
TREKKING IN MERCILESS SUN AND THIRST

DECEMBER 3, 1943

Kawanishi awoke at the campsite near the coast from a dream-filled night, his body hurting at the slightest movement. Everyone needed a day of rest and by luck, they had stumbled into a beautiful spot. "Bands of sunlight poured through the gaps of trees towering high above the jungle floor, covering us in a delicate and intricate tapestry of light. It was magnificent, like sitting in a massive Gothic cathedral." Twice enemy aircraft flew overhead and now that they were on the coast, it became important to remain under cover in broad daylight. At dusk, they moved out. As they trudged toward the coast, the ground hardened and walking got easier. Darkness fell and blinking fireflies appeared.

The fireflies reminded Kawanishi of days in Setagaya when he and his sisters would catch fireflies on the banks of the Karasuyama Reservoir. Their "cool greenish-white halo" would flicker as if they were breathing. Some fell into the water still shining. It brought back the smell of bamboo grass and of summer. Absorbed in childhood memories, Kawanishi lost himself in solitary reverie. But soon enough, reality imposed itself.

> We halted the column at 2000. It wasn't possible to go any further. But here deep in the mountains the road had turned into a complete morass and there was no place to

sit down. We selected a sharp incline on the edge of the road where water hadn't collected and literally collapsed. Water was seeping through my clothes but still I didn't move. I just stared into black space for a while. A swarm of ravenous mosquitoes attacked us.

I could feel the murky water as it slowly worked its way through my clothes. It brought on terrible dreams and along with the marauding mosquitoes made for a night of shallow sleep. Here in the primeval jungle, pitch black, deep in mud, all 270 of us passed the night like abandoned dogs.

The next day:

We followed the road down the mountain and entered another palm tree plantation. One felt a sense of security when walking on the hard sand of these shoreline plantations. Here, we took a short break. Fallen coconuts were scattered everywhere. The laborers raced to be the first to pick them up and immediately started cutting them open.

Some split the 50 to 60-centimeter coconuts open, poured out the milk, and ate the cottony fiber of the fruit. Some ate the copra of young coconuts that tastes somewhat like squid. And still others cut open a hole and drank the milk. There were more than enough to go around. The laborers were in paradise eating and drinking to their hearts' content.

The sun was merciless. It was all we could do to not throw off the 20-kilogram-plus packs digging into our shoulders. I was thirsty, my breath dry. My canteen was already empty. We walked on through the blinding glare of the mountain meadow. It was almost 1000—enemy aircraft might come any minute. If our column of 270 laborers were caught out here, there would be no place to hide. We had to get across this grassy hillside as fast as possible. I prodded laborers who had fallen out of the column to get up and keep a move on, and I forced myself to do the same.

As I walked at the head of the column, I suddenly heard the sound of water coming from around the next bend. I hurried ahead and discovered water gushing out of the mountain from a small drainpipe. I couldn't believe it. I turned around and shouted, "Water!" and started gulping it down.

The word "water" made its way through the column like a whirlwind. Even men who had been unable to walk grasped their staffs and staggered to their feet. I worked my way to the back, telling everyone there was water ahead, and to line up for a drink and then keep moving. I told them to hang on, we were almost there. Hearing this, the laborers climbed the mountain road wearing looks of joy and anticipation on their faces.

I went back to the spout and found chaos. Men were fighting to drink at the same time and trying to drink before the man ahead of him was finished. Some were even trying to stick in their mouths at the point where the pipe jutted out of the rock. Men were falling all over each other. It was completely out of control, a near riot. Men were fighting like crazed animals for their sip of water. Some were even trying to slurp it up from the muddy stream at their feet.

I had to bring these men back to order. Pushing a couple of men out of my way, I forced my way toward the spout, grabbed it, and struck the man drinking. At that, the laborers fell silent and shuffled into line as if the utter pandemonium of just seconds earlier had never happened.

We still hadn't eaten breakfast. We took a break at this spot, and I ordered the men to prepare their meals. Finally, I had some time to myself. I threw my rucksack onto the grass, pulled out a little bottle of whisky, shoved it into my pocket, and leisurely headed back toward the

*plaza we had just crossed. I cleared a space among some
vines around my feet and lay down a little bit to the side
of the road. Alone and at ease, I let myself relax and took
a drink of whisky.*

*I love a good drink. The whisky was a special gift
to me from the chief paymaster at 8th Fleet Headquarters
upon my departure from Buin. I held the brown bottle
up to the light and saw that only a little bit was left. I
took off the cap, filled it with whisky, and slowly drank,
savoring the flavor. I felt a pleasant burning sensation in
my throat as it made its way to my stomach. As I finished
off the last of it, I thought about how the attachments I
had formed at Buin had been so suddenly cut off. I threw
the empty bottle as hard as I could into the jungle. The
bottle glittered in the sunlight as it tumbled through the
air and then vanished in the jungle. A bit tipsy, I lay
down and enjoyed the breeze blowing in from the ocean.*

That Kawanishi had a small store of liquor amid such scarcity
is not surprising. Drinking serious quantities of *sake* or whisky was
an accepted way of life in the Imperial Japanese Navy. All night *sake*
parties among the officers were common. In fact, these practices
mirrored society where drunks were tolerated, even encouraged. When
Kawanishi arrived at his future father-in-law's house after the war to
ask for his daughter's hand in marriage, he was intoxicated. In most
societies, this would pose a problem, but here the two went out drinking
the rest of the night. Not only did Kawanishi receive permission to
marry the daughter but was asked to take the family name, Fujimoto.

US Navy regulations, on the other hand, prohibited drinking
alcohol on board ship, a rule that often was quietly ignored. In fact,
the scotch-drinking Jannotta at one point stretched the regulations and
he got called on the carpet by Admiral Halsey. He, too, enjoyed his
whisky. Kawanishi went on:

*A soldier came around looking for me. I stood up and
yelled "hello" and he ran over and told me that one of the*

126

*men was seriously ill. He was the big fellow who had been
stricken with malaria when we were going through the
mountains along the coast. We had managed to get him
this far but we didn't have the strength to take him any
farther. I decided there was no choice but to leave him in
the care of the local army garrison.*

*We cut down some small trees and fashioned a
stretcher. Eight of us took turns carrying him to the army
huts situated halfway up Koromira Mountain. I explained
the situation to the Lieutenant in command and he
graciously took responsibility for the sick man. His kindness
was a real lift to my spirits. He asked us to take him to the
field hospital on a nearby slope.*

*The road up the slope to the field hospital was a
zigzagging log stairway. A soldier on his way down to fetch
water stopped and gave a crisp salute. I felt like I had just
returned to the military after a long absence. It was a good
feeling. We rested twice on the way and eventually made it
to the field hospital. In the hut, the sick were laid out on
beds made from betel nut palm.*

*I pestered the medic over and over to take good care
of the sick laborer. The medic gave him a shot, and I said,
"Get better and join us later! There's another group coming
by in a few days." But I knew he wouldn't recover that
soon. It really weighed on my conscience to leave this man
behind in his condition. I trudged down the hill with a
heavy heart.*

Before again getting under way, Kawanishi found a navy
communication team and sent a message: "Passed through Koromira
at noon on December 4th. Five men are ill, left one at army garrison
here." They had to make Kieta that night and he ordered the men out.

*Yet again, we entered the narrow path winding its way
like a tunnel through the jungle, but my body would
go no further. Did I even manage to walk at all? I was*

127

beyond the edge of exhaustion. My mouth couldn't form words. Here, in this pitch-black jungle, blacker than the darkest night, gasping desperately for breath, we fell to the ground in our tracks and sank into deep, deep sleep in the muddy mire.

December 5, 1943

Morning. 0400. Drifting fog in the faint morning light. My uniform is completely damp from night dew. I'm cold. My feet are swollen and numb in gaiters I haven't taken off in days. I lay motionless, my eyes wide open. I wanted more than anything to just stay right where I was and sleep forever—I wanted to arrive at Kieta before breakfast where the navy had a detachment. There the sick could rest and everyone could replenish their rations. But what I wanted more than anything was to get us out of this hellish jungle as soon as possible.

We descended a steep road as jagged as a bolt of lightening. At the bottom, we crossed a pebble-strewn riverbed with razor-sharp grass. A crudely built zigzag bridge was suspended over the water. We crossed the bridge and came to a log bridge suspended over a rock-covered field. We formed into a long column and crossed it single file.

The opposite bank had to be the outskirts of Kieta. It felt good to walk on the two-meter wide road of packed sand flanked by a canopy of palms and croton. I could see a cluster of native dwellings. Certainly, a few native children lived here as well. My mood gradually brightened and I forget the exhaustion I'd been enduring nonstop over the last several days.

At 0900, we stopped to rest at the edge of a scrub forest and tighten up our column, which had gotten very spread out. Just then, I heard the sound of distant explosions heading our way. It was a bombing run by a large aircraft formation. I immediately ordered the whole unit to camouflage their packs with foliage and then scatter and hide in the jungle.

The formation continued coming in our direction and soon flew overhead with a deafening roar. Through the treetops, I could see the bellies of 50 or 60 bombers, the ordnance on their bellies clearly visible through the jungle foliage. But right now bombers weren't our biggest threat —our circumstances made us far more terrified of being strafed by fighters.

The formation flew down the coastline. I pushed my way through head-high grass to the edge of the jungle. I panned the coastline with my eyes. Like a great swarm of flies, I saw the planes flying far off in the distance. Suddenly, they broke formation. Looking through my field glasses, I clearly saw that they had started a bombing run. I could see them diving one after another so clearly that I thought I could reach out and touch them.

I remembered that yesterday the communications unit at Koromira had said that the bombing there for the last few days had been really bad. What's more, I had believed that aid awaited us at Kieta. With this in mind, I had encouraged the sick among us, rallied them on despite their exhaustion. But now I knew that Kieta would offer us no such sanctuary. The exhilaration of a moment before was instantly crushed by despair. It was dark by 1600. We got ready to move out for another miserable night of marching. We walked for a time along the shore under rows of low palm trees, the sound of crashing waves in our ears. Then the road headed into the jungle. Silently, I concentrated my feet and moved forward a step at a time. Each man was on his own, completely isolated from his fellows by the absolute darkness enshrouding us. We'd take a 5 minute break every 15 minutes to tighten up the column. After taking roll, we'd start moving again, my command to move out the only sound piercing the morbidly oppressive gloom.

There's no sense of distance when marching in total darkness, so it was hard to know how far we'd walked, but my watch showed that it was now past 2100. We finally made it to Kieta at 0100 in the morning. I could see the town under the moonlight. The governor general of Bougainville had lived here. I saw the red roofs of Western-style buildings and a 10-meter-wide road skirting along the coast. Offshore, the black outline of Bakawari Island loomed in the darkness. Kieta was known for its beautiful scenery. The beach road reminded me of the driveway of a summer resort. Gentle waves lapped the beach. At last, we were at Kieta. The prospect of getting here was the only thing that had kept us going. The idyllic scenery now before me seemed like a whole other world.

I went to see the garrison commander. A non-commissioned officer showed me to his quarters, a wooden building whose painted walls in the moonlight looked like blue water. We passed under an arch of bougainvillea, crossed a stone walkway and climbed steps to a room on the second floor. Perhaps it had been the home of a Chinese merchant. The doors and walls were in a Chinese style. The end of a dark corridor suddenly opened into a large room lit by lamplight. The air was damp and the out-of-date Chinese décor gave the place a bizarre ambience. The young officer left and I waited there alone. I stared at the dim lamp and let its faint heat warm my spirit. Its light instinctively calmed my physically and emotionally exhausted body.

A lieutenant appeared, an older man with white in his hair. He looked clearly irritated at having his sleep interrupted. Holding a lamp in both hands, he entered the room without a word and plopped down into a chair. He blurted out, "Well done," and then resumed his silence.

With the shadow of his silhouette dancing on a fluttering Chinese curtain, and without a trace of emotion in his glum expression, he listened as I forced out the words

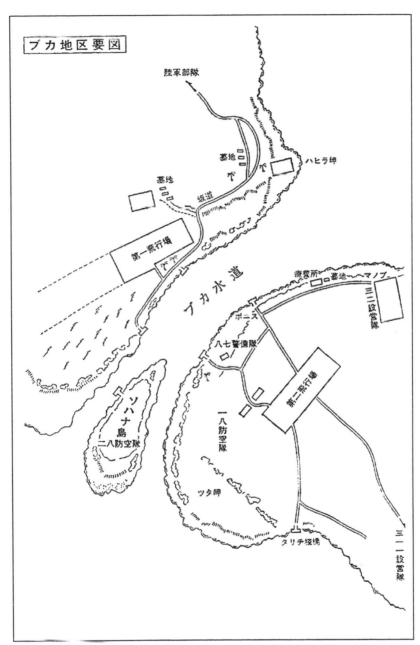

Sketch of Buka Island and the northern coast of Bougainville Island from Kawanishi's book, *Records of Wars*.

describing our journey so far and my desire to receive rest and care for the exhausted laborers. When I finished, he said that since there had been air raids over the last several days and the enemy might land at any time, offering any aid was out of the question. He then coldly asserted that their bomb shelters couldn't fit that many men anyhow so it would in fact be better if we departed Kieta that very night.

He regarded us as nothing more than an uninvited nuisance.

I looked at him and said nothing. I felt a deep surge of contempt for this man. He looked away from me as he spoke and at the lamp instead. His expression left no doubt that we wouldn't be given even the slightest amount of his unit's food or medicine. At that moment I came to know the utter and complete coldness at the heart of the military—I felt it all the way down to my bones. For me—someone who had come up through the comfortable confines of headquarters, and who even then was a student and a gentleman—this was truly repugnant. I resolved to ask nothing of him, and I considered leaving Kieta at dawn.

I got a telegraph form and wrote out a message under the lamplight: "December 6, 0200 hours. Passed through Kieta. Left three. No dead. Ensign Kawanishi."

I went back to the men, now asleep on the side of the road. Knowing that I would have to lead these men through Kieta without providing them any aid or pleasure stirred in me a determination to fight on. I asked the local unit's non-commissioned officer to wake us at 0400 and lay down on my canvas.

I remembered the sudden look of delight on the old lieutenant's face when I said I'd ask nothing of him. In an effort to wipe the image out of my mind, I shook my head and looked up at the sky. Above were beautiful stars in a nearly moonless sky.

December 6, 1943

Since Kieta was a bombing target, Kawanishi, after sleeping "what felt like five or six minutes," moved his men out to put distance between them and the base. They followed the shore line for two hours and took a break in an area between the sea and the edge of the jungle.

Here and there, the laborers formed into groups of 10 or so and settled in to enjoy the day of rest. They flopped down and crossed their legs, some gnawing on dried bread as if they had died and gone to heaven. For a while, I watched these men as they relaxed both with fondness and with regret at the travails I had put them through. I took off my gaiters and hung them on a branch in the sunlight. After that, I lost any desire to do anything at all. I stretched out on my lumpy canvas. All was quiet except for the noise the laborers made as they moved about. Before I knew it, I had fallen into a deep sleep.

A few minutes later, I became aware of a thunderous roar all around me. Gut instinct roused me from the depths of sleep and I opened my eyes. Though I had only been asleep for a short while, for a few moments I was in a daze, unsure of what I was dreaming and what was real. A deafening roar engulfed the area. Enemy planes came into view in the sky above.

"Take cover! Hit the dirt!" I yelled, but the roar of the planes was so loud that I couldn't hear my own words. I hugged the ground. While I had been asleep, the laborers had hung a mosquito net over me to keep off the sun. Somehow, I imagined the net as a solid barrier, I crawled up to its hem. I was so disoriented that I thought doing so would give me an extra margin of safety. I raised my head and futilely screamed, "Nobody move!"

What seemed like a great distance after we left Kieta and walked all night through the mountains turned out to be not far at all as the crow flies. We had marched with such desperation that we thought we had gotten quite far from Kieta, but we were still nearby.

Another round of explosions started; a second time they headed our way. We had to face this attack in broad daylight, in grass that offered only the barest cover, and with no weapons to defend ourselves. I was gripped by terror. The boom of exploding bombs was followed by a body-shaking thump. The ground trembled, the grass seemed to be swept away as if by a giant hand. I clung to the ground, dripping with sweat. I remember suddenly wanting to scream.

The air filled with the sound of explosions and destruction. I saw the landscape transform before my eyes as the force of blasts smashed and tore apart huge trees and rocky precipices. We found ourselves increasingly exposed to sunlight. We clung on helplessly—all we could do was hang on for dear life.

The number of explosions decreased. I could hear Kieta being strafed off in the distance. The bombing where we were had ended. The last explosion was in a palm tree grove along the coast, after that the explosions gradually grew more distant. The whole area was inundated with the pungent odor of gunpowder and tree sap.

In a daze, I stared blankly at the jungle landscape around me. I saw an alien world populated with bizarre insects—huge red ants and caterpillar-like creatures crowned with shells on their backs—crawling over a thick bed of dead and rotting leaves built up over the eons. As I looked uncomprehendingly at this scene, I gradually came back to my senses.

In the next instant, the workers began moving about. We had to do roll call. After roll, the half dozen or so squad leaders—their faces still showing the terror they had experienced minutes ago—came to me. Miraculously, despite the intensity of the bombing no one was hurt. I was *so relieved that I started to laugh. I said, "I bet you weren't expecting a wake up call like that, eh!" They all started to laugh too and talked about what a strange scene the whole thing had made. After we talked for awhile, I said we should get some more sleep and we headed back into the jungle that served as our bed.*

As Kawanishi thought back on the morning's bombing, he had been told to expect two bombing attacks —one in the morning and one in the afternoon—and now they needed to get somewhere safe before the afternoon raid. He forced his body to its feet and ordered everyone to move out at once. And as he looked back along a ridge, he saw observation pillboxes that had antiaircraft emplacements. "We had taken a break right on Kieta's defensive perimeter! This had happened due to our poor maps, along with being too exhausted to notice." Their next goal was Arawa where a one-week supply of food awaited them.

US sailors and soldiers on liberty in Australia. *Australian War Memorial*

Chapter XV

LIBERTY

USS LCI L 328
December 26, 1943, Florida Is., Solomons

My Darling,

Since we were back "at home" in our base port, we all had what fun could be had for Xmas. There was a swell USO show—3 men and two movies—Xmas Eve. Christmas Day, all ships had turkey dinner. In the afternoon the officers gathered at an "open house" by Commander Smith, who had just moved into his new quarters built ashore. It's the best in this whole area—perched on a mountain overlooking the bay where we anchor all our ships—a glorious view and cool breezes. Officers from the cruiser, destroyers, LSTs were there in addition to our own outfit—including one Admiral. The first and only party and real relaxation any of us have had since we left Noumea last May.

Wazo (Comdr. Byrd) wasn't there—he's on his way back now from Australia. Incidentally, CDR Smith and I got quite a surprise a couple of days ago. Orders came in for Wazo to return to the US for one month's leave and new assignment to duty. I say it was a surprise because we had made up our minds Tactical Unit Commanders (group or flotilla) were pretty much stuck out here for the duration. But it opens possibilities—maybe I'll get orders back in a few months. I don't allow myself to hope too much, but there's a chance, apparently. I received another surprise today. It was a copy of a dispatch sent by Commander Landing Craft Flotillas Admiral Forte to Commander LCI L Flotilla Five CDR Smith, "Desire LCDR Jannotta in a command and take eight LCIs to Sydney for two weeks' recreation leaving January one." So, this evening we had another drawing of ship numbers to see which ones would go. My flagship was not drawn—Byrd's was—so I can't take the old 328 with me. I'll have to use the 61 as my flagship. The ships that go with me are four of my group, three of Byrd's, one of Rankin's. So my group came out pretty lucky. It's a 1,700-mile jaunt each way, and we'll have two weeks there, so we'll be gone about a month. It's a great break and will do all officers and men much good. All hands are quite excited.

I hope I can get some letters from you before I leave because our mail won't be forwarded to us, and it'll be another four or more weeks before we get back.

Maybe I can send you a cable from Australia. They say you can.

Well, darling girl, a new year starts pretty soon. I hope, more than anything in the world, it will bring us together again.

Vernon

———※※※———

USS LCI L 61
At Sea, January 6, 1944

My Darling,

Well, here we are, actually on our way for a two weeks' leave in Sydney, Australia. We've been at sea for five days now and are due to arrive there in the morning of January 8.

I have eight LCIs with me and, besides the 40 officers and 240 men comprising the ships' crews, I have an additional 20 officers and 60 men from the Admiral's staff, CDR Smith's staff, and other amphibious force staffs who are ordered to me for temporary duty for the purpose of giving them leave, also.

I had much running around to do before we left because, of course, I didn't get my final orders until about 48 hours before we were due to leave and I had to get all ships fueled, watered, provisioned, last minute repairs, etc. All three of the ships which I was taking with me didn't get back to the base from mission until 24 hours before sailing time. The Admiral finally agreed to let me make the cruise direct from Guadalcanal to Australia instead of via Noumea, New Caledonia, and go without escort. Saves time.

Everyone aboard all ships was pretty excited and feeling pretty good when we got under way and filed out of the harbor last Saturday. In spite of four days of very bad weather, high winds, rough seas, and rains, all are in fine spirits. The weather broke today and the sea is quite calm.

It does seem strange that we will actually be away from the combat area, and on our own, for five weeks—three weeks at sea and two weeks in Sydney. Back to civilization again. All of us have received plenty of information on where to go, what to do, addresses of families and girls, from the men who made the cruise before us, and from other ships. CDR Byrd and several officers on our cruisers (which were there in November) have given me all the information I need to assure men and officers getting the most of their time there, and the addresses of three families to be sure to contact myself.

CDR Byrd has now gone back to the States, so have Townsend, Maxie and McCoy (three of my best COs), for leave, and then to bring out new ships. I lose four more of my skippers this month—same way. Have replaced all with men who have served on the ships as junior officers and they are all good boys and doing fine.

I have two of our gunboats with me, and one of them has really had a great deal of trouble—engine breakdowns, etc. She had had a long tour of duty at Bougainville and came back the day before we left without any chance for overhaul. She has slowed me down so I'll be a day late getting in. I had originally planned to make it on the 7th. The foul weather made it tougher, but we'll make it OK day after tomorrow.

They say we can send a cable—but no mail or souvenirs—from Australia, so as soon as I get in I'll cable you. Let me know if and when you get it. I will file it from Sydney on February 8.

Well, Darling, I'll have to get back to the bridge again—that's where I spend the larger part of my days and nights when at sea.

I love you, Sweetheart, and miss you and the girls very, very much. All my love to all of you.

There is no letter to his wife recording Jannotta's liberty experience in Sydney; but his mess steward, Amos Milburn, whom Jannotta considered "intelligent, and gay, and funny," wrote to Jannotta late in the war and recalled his time on leave there. His letters give a glimpse of the celebration they had in Australia.

February 28, 1945
Pacific Area

Dear Commander:

How are you? I am well and doing fine. I am still stewardsmate first class. As you know ships in amphibious forces don't rate third class officers cook or steward.

I had a wonderful time at home on my leave with my folks, thanks to you. When I was home I told everyone about you, what a wonderful guy you were. I was stationed in Galveston for two months and then shipped out again on LSM 319. Commander, I shall never forget the times we spent together, our ships coming in and beaching at Hutchinson's Creek in the Solomon Islands back in 1943, movies at Carter City, and also the Fourth of July, 1943. I still say you are one of the bravest men ever lived.

Even Australia, what a wonderful time we had there. I will never forget the Countess Elizabeth. And Ensign Potts and the redhead. What a party we had that night and what good eats and drinks. I still remember what you said about if you ever ran across me out there you would take me with you again. Oh yes, I broke two microphones and two pianos in Panama. How is Mrs. Jannotta?

How do you like your new stewards mate? Is he better than I was? Ask him to write to me. I am advancing a lot faster in age now. I will be 18 the first of April. Do you still drink your coffee, cream and no sugar, and your eggs sunny side up? And I know you still like your sardines.

Well, Commander, I will have to close now. Will be looking forward to hearing from you soon. I wish you the very best of luck with the group of ships you now take command over, and may God bless you and send us all home safely.

Hope to see you soon.

Amos Milburn Jr. Stm 1/c

P.S. I am a wizard of a signalman now. Sure wish I could get the rate.

The US Navy in WWII was mostly a white man's affair with only a few rates (naval ranks) open to blacks. President Truman changed that in the summer of 1948 with an executive order to end discrimination in the armed forces.

US Navy LCI L ships unloading men at Morotai, September 15, 1944. *US Army*

Chapter XVI
RAMP-UP: NEW AND IMPROVED LCI Ls

December 5, 1943
Florida Island, Solomons

My Sweetheart:

I've been busy, and so has the whole flotilla staff, getting these new ships (LCI Ls) ready for action. They landed here loaded to the hilt with replacement men and officers for our LCIs and for other ships and naval units up here and with cargo of all kinds for a couple of dozen different ships; bases, or units, running from engine spares and parts to gun spares, personal gear and special consignments. I had to get that straightened out first (the replacements distributed to half a dozen different bases for further distribution) the same with the cargo, then strip the ships and crew of everything they didn't need to have on board with which to operate or live on, store it in our warehouses ashore, then get started on all necessary hull and engine repairs, get them painted with our special tropical green camouflage, mount some additional guns on them, load them with proper ammunition, get their compasses compensated, fuel, water, and provision them. The officers and crews look like a fine bunch of men. They handle their ships well, and apparently had good basic training before leaving the States. Their spirit is excellent. They are proud of their ships, of being in the amphibious forces, a part of our flotilla (we have a good reputation), and they are eager for action. Well, I expect they'll get it soon enough. I'm taking one of the new ones with me among the others tomorrow and will transfer my flag to it, temporarily, for this particular mission.

In addition to much-needed personnel replacements for casualties, they brought us a consignment of 68 replacements for petty officers to be sent back to the States for new ships being constructed. So, in addition to having to release all commanding officers for new ships, we are going to have to release all of our experienced petty officers, about 400 of them, over the next six months. Of course we've been training and breaking in non-rated men to replace them, but that's a pretty heavy turnover of the backbone of our organization, and it's going to mean much work and effort to see it through. It's a sensible program, though, and we'll make out all right. Of course all these officers and petty officers going, or to go, back to the States as nucleus crews for the new ships, will get some leave in the States (2 to 4 weeks) before reporting to their ships. We're sending our best men—not getting rid of our dubs—and so this has given great stimuli to work and morale among the crews.

As unit commanders, flotilla and group commanders, we stay here, and absorb and fit the new ships into our units as they come out and are assigned to us. We won't be returned to the States for new commands. We are expected to stick it out and see it all the way through with the Pacific Forces. However, CDR Smith told me the other day that by next summer he and I (he didn't mention Byrd or Rankin, perhaps because they weren't present) should be able to get a 30-day leave in the States with air transportation both ways. Well, that's something to look forward to at any rate. I will have been out here over 18 months by then, and can honestly feel I'm entitled to leave, if to no change of duty, by then.

We can't count on it, Darling, but at least it's something for which we can have strong hopes. Maybe we could celebrate your birthday together, or our wedding anniversary, Nicky's birthday, or all three. Wouldn't that be something? And would I be glad to see you.

My own Sweetheart—you know all that's in my heart to tell you when I say simply, "I love you".

—◦◦◦—

Dealing with the Realities at Hand

Kawanishi had been marching for a week now, and except for painful feet blisters, his men grew accustomed to the trekking. He wrote:

On arriving at Arawa Bay, I felt as happy as a man on Sunday. After contacting the hospital and local army unit, I had two men accompany me down a path toward the ocean in search of the base. Along the way, I could see squash gardens that soldiers had planted on gently sloping ground. We passed under papaya trees, something I hadn't done for a long time. Under the cliff of a sharp hill a dense cluster of trees extended well over the water. Here, two motor boats (containing supplies) had been moored in a well-concealed cove.

After a while, it was time to eat. I ate with gusto the first rice I'd had in a while. We had just replenished our supplies and still had plenty to eat. The time slipped by. The day had passed without us encountering any enemy air patrols.

We moved out at 1500. Our pace is always brisk for the first two or three hours after starting, and we move twice as fast in the day compared to marching at night. 1500 was almost dusk in the South Seas and I was enjoying the increasing chill in the air as we walked. Suddenly, a report came from the rear of the column: one of the men had collapsed. I stopped the march and went to the rear

145

to see what was up. I encountered a young Korean worker writing in the grass, his squad leader, an older man, standing nearby.

Many of the 270 men Kawanishi led were Korean. In the highly structured Japanese society, the Koreans ranked at the bottom of the hierarchy. Typically, pay in a Japanese factory rewarded the Koreans at one-third the wages of a Japanese worker performing the same tasks. Treated as an inferior race and discriminated against economically and socially, the Koreans lived on the edge of Japanese society.

"What's wrong?" I asked. "Before moving out he said his appendix hurt, but because we were all heading back to Rabaul he wanted to go, too," said the squad leader. My immediate impulse was to scream, "You idiot! Why didn't you say anything about your physical situation before departure?" But that wouldn't have solved the problem. I thought about how the young man must have felt in the face of being left, separated from his comrades, in a place where his fate was uncertain at best. It made sense for him to lie his way into joining us on this desperate march. The worker, who looked to be only 16 or so, was in agony. I wondered what to do. If he had only let us know the day before we could have had an army doctor look at him, but what now?

I looked at this boy as he suffered—his body contorted as a shrimp, his face a deathly pallor—and I felt so angry at his foolishness and fed up by my helplessness that I just stood there speechless. If we stayed here, we'd deplete our rations. We had only 6 days of food and no idea of what difficulties lay ahead. Since everyone was now carrying a full load of rations, having others carry the boy would slow down our pace. We wouldn't be able to march at night, either. And I knew from what happened at Koromira that carrying him risked greatly increasing our casualties.

Should I just abandon a sick man in this jungle

146

wilderness? Abandon a boy who suppressed his illness because he wanted more than anything to return to Rabaul? The laborers sat in the grass waiting. The day continued to fade. Casting my eyes over the sea, I stood mutely in the face of such awful circumstances. I turned my eyes from the bright sea. I pondered how to abandon this pitiable youth in a way that would fool my conscience.

"Who's this man's squad leader?" An old boat captain, already past 50, came forward. "Your group will wait here. Follow us after he recovers a bit." The old boat captain looked at me, his expression pleading, desperate. Leaving seven men behind with a sick man in this jungle wilderness could mean death for them all. In particular, they might not be able to stand the isolation and fear. I knew this, but there was no other way that would at least momentarily satisfy my conscience. I wanted to bury my face in my hands. I was well aware that I was deceiving my conscience by risking the lives of seven men by leaving them behind to tend to a single sick man.

The boat captain, an elderly and good-natured man I had known ever since I had arrived in Rabaul, spoke to me in his halting Japanese. He said he told the man to stay behind from the moment we left Buin, but he came anyway so this is his fault. He said leaving his commander after making it this far was out of the question, and besides he was too old to look after someone else anyway.

Convinced that death was his only other alternative, this old man had walked over 200 kilometers at the side of younger men. When we had left Buin he had an old winter coat and some other things from back home, but by now he had discarded everything heavy he had brought with him. Betting everything on making it back alive, he carried nothing but his rucksack of food, wore nothing but a blanket and ragged shirt, and supported himself with a branch of wood he used as a staff. The deep wrinkles in his face, his white hair, were the face of a man who had spent many years of his life at sea. And now, after all this, the boat captain was standing here saying these pitiable and cruel words to me. He was absolutely determined to survive. It was clear to me that I couldn't leave this old man here.

It grew dark as the magnificent South Seas twilight descended. I once again asked the sick man if he was able to walk. The youth, covered in sweat, didn't move in response. I had to make a decision. Half-measures to assuage my conscience were unacceptable. No matter how awful I found this life and death dilemma to be I had to give an order.

I ordered two young and strong men in his squad to stay behind with him and then take him to the nearest army base when he had recovered enough. The two could then join the third group of laborers scheduled to depart in about a week. Their faces turned pale, but before they could say anything—before they could tell me how they had suffered, how they had struggled to come this far—I said, "That's an order!" I gave them double rations and medicine and ordered the rest of us to move out. I told these men over and over that the third group would be passing through in a week. I walked to the head of our column. The fireflies would soon be rising from the swamp and taking to the air. We had to move out.

I hadn't abandoned the man.

The trek from this point was, like the first half, a continuous struggle against hardship, except that our legs and bodies were now so accustomed to marching that they moved almost mechanically and our spirits had become increasingly resilient. I no longer fell into sentimental brooding and feelings of regret: I simply dealt with the reality at hand. After experiencing how inefficient and exhausting night marches were, I increasingly had us march in daytime while avoiding the hours most likely to encounter enemy aircraft.

Between Arigutsu and the army base at Numa Numa lay the abandoned village of Tepeloi. They had already crossed three dangerous rivers without a mishap since the trek began and they now faced another. Their map showed a stream en route to the village, but instead they discovered a broad river bed more than 200 meters wide.

> *It was almost 0800, the river bed glittered brightly. The current was fairly swift. It would be too much trouble to remove our uniforms at this time of day, so we entered and began wading across the river bed still wearing them.*
>
> *Just then, with our hands joined in chest deep water, a squadron of enemy planes appeared moving over the ocean. There was no way we could react—everyone just watched the squadron frozen in place. Fortunately, for us, the squadron appeared to be on the way to making an attack on Buka as it was heading north and not our way. Terrified by what would happen to us were we to be strafed during our journey, we ran full tilt for the cover of jungle.*

At this point, they had completed two-thirds of the trek. The laborers seemed to sense that the worst was over and now trusted Kawanishi completely. "I steadily became more used to the fighting. My nerves steadied. I became more self-confident at commanding the laborers and could make sound decisions quickly. The trek required one more significant push to reach their destination. Everyone was filled with optimism."

> *At Teopanno, we received a second resupply of rations.*
>
> *It was December 17—we had been marching for 17 days. As we got closer to Buka, in high spirits everyone picked up the pace.*
>
> *On the morning of December 18, we quickly set off for Bonis and our final day of marching on a three-meter wide road through a palm grove. We broke into a brisk trot. We had lunch near Sorum. While taking a break in a patch of sparse vegetation a truck came by. We had reached*

Buka, but I didn't know where headquarters was located so I stopped the truck to inquire. Seeing an actual motor vehicle was thrilling—it had been so long since we had seen something from the civilized world. The sight caused a commotion among the laborers. We've really made it, I thought. The truck belonged to the 32nd Construction Unit. I decided to use the time while everyone was resting to ride the truck to headquarters so I could report on our trek and find out what we needed to do next. I told the men I'd be back soon and hopped on the truck.

The truck lurched sharply left and right on the terrible road. Fifteen minutes later, we arrived at a palm grove on a cliff above headquarters. I descended the 30-meter cliff to some caves where 87th Garrison headquarters were located. Captain Ikeda was there. He complimented me for a job well done for such a trying assignment.

Then I asked Captain Eikichi Kato, the garrison commander, about what we should do next. His response devastated me. During our 18 days of marching, the fighting had gone badly. The enemy now patrolled the waters so closely that it was no longer possible to send out any motorized-sailing boats or motor boats even at night. Only a fraction of the 13th Construction Unit, which had arrived before us, made it to Rabaul.

I thought of everything that these 270 men—spurred on only by the hope of making it home—had endured during our 18-day march. Now that hope, too, had vanished completely. What would I tell them? I was too shocked to speak.

Then Captain Kato said, "We'll put up your men and the remainder of the 13th in temporary barracks. We'll have the sailors in transport and munitions stay near headquarters. New barracks will be built for them in the palm grove up on the cliff." All I could think about was how to break this awful news to the 270 men who even now were ecstatically dreaming about their return home.

These 270 men and I had suffered much together and I cared about them deeply. I didn't know what to do. Finally I said, "Yes, sir," and started to leave. Captain Kato and Captain Ikeda then asked where my men were. I told them they were resting at Sorum. Kato said, "We'll tell them the news. It's closer for you to go straight to the 32nd barracks from here. You look tired so rest here awhile." I said I couldn't because they were all waiting for me. Still, I worried whether I had the courage to tell them. I could already imagine their faces when I break the terrible news.

Captain Ikeda said, "Your assignment was to bring these 270 men here and now it is finished. Your duties are with munitions and transport so there's no need for you to go back to them." I had been standing the whole time. They now offered me a chair and I sat down. Suddenly, my intense fatigue, the emotional shock, hit me all at once. I was too tired to care—whatever happens, happens.

I had a message sent to 8th Fleet: "December 18, 1200. Arrived in Buka. Of the 270, 4 left behind to join third group." While the message was being sent, a junior officer was summoned and told to go and deliver the news to the men at Sorum. I watched silently as he was given his order. I didn't want to part in this way with the laborers with whom I had shared so much hardship. I sat there, torn between my desire to go back and see them and say farewell and having to give them such terrible news, as they handled the problem like it was nothing more than another office chore. My exhaustion overwhelmed me and I fell asleep in the chair.

A Japanese working party loading rations onto Japanese barges for transport and distribution to troops in the Buka area. *Australian War Memorial*

Chapter XVII

SUBMARINE RESUPPLY

BUKA, DECEMBER 24, 1943

Several days after completing the trek up Bougainville to Buka, Kawanishi visited the men he had led. He found them devastated, "piteously calling, 'Captain, Captain' begging me to do something but there was nothing I could do to make things better for them. In the end, less than 20 of the 270 men would live to go home." At the supply branch, Kawanishi was assigned to a group responsible for the management of the supplies coming to the island. But by late December 1943, Allied Forces so dominated the sea and air around Bougainville that the tight blockade cut off Buka and the 7,000 Japanese forces there from almost all resupply. The food inventories, already critical, became desperate, and Kawanishi wrote, "it sent the Buka area plunging toward starvation". In a last-ditch effort to get food, Captain Kato, commander of the 87th Garrison, pressed Rabaul for shipments of supplies by submarine. Several night attempts were made but each time the sub was discovered by Allied aircraft and the mission aborted. Finally, it was decided to send a small submarine. Kawanishi, assigned to plan and carry out the rendezvous, tells the story:

Because we feared a night attack by enemy planes above all else, the submarine would surface for only 15 minutes. We worked hard preparing to unload under this constraint. Logistics had four motor boats. To unload as much as possible within the 15-minute time span, we made a slide with ropes on one end to tie to the submarine and slide supplies down to the boats. Submarine decks are slippery and hard to walk on, so instead of shoes or jikatabi—*socks with rubber soles—we made canvas shoes. While unloading we would turn off the boat engines so as not to make waves and keep flashlight use to a minimum. Our motor boats were fragile so we immediately inspected them and resolved to avoid damaging them in any way on the day the shipment arrived. We decided how many men to have on the deck of the submarine and how many below receiving supplies. We drilled countless times, making adjustments each time.*

Ultimately, it all came down to those 15 minutes. The commotion we made bringing all this together during the several days remaining until the appointed day had the air of battle preparations. Even the smallest mistake would spoil the plan. Still, even with all this careful preparation, we discovered damage to one of the boats just before we were to go out and meet the submarine; the boat set off with not a moment to spare.

On the appointed night, four boats lay hidden below a northern Bougainville cliff just off the Buka channel. Suddenly, the men aboard spotted a dark object with "one speck of a light" moving to the rendezvous point. Kawanishi continued:

The submarine stopped and the boats moved next to it. We couldn't get on deck because of the rough sea, so the sub's crew helped a couple of our men get on board. The darkness made it difficult to find my way about with only a flashlight. What I saw once I got on board the sub shocked me. The rice included on the list of items was in sealed, half-full plastic bags that had been brought out on deck and covered in large sheets of canvas. By the time I got on deck, the crew had already removed the canvas and had begun tossing the bags of rice onto the boats. Since we had been unable to meet and discuss details with the sub's crew in advance, things started out in much greater confusion than expected.

Nonetheless, we formed a chain to quickly relay the 13mm and 20mm ammunition, medicine and other supplies through the sub's narrow hatch. The slide proved very useful for this. Wanting to finish as fast as possible, our work pace built to a fever pitch. The sub's rolling made working difficult. The strong waves tossed our boats away from the sub and then back against it. Some of the bags of rice fell into the sea, but there was nothing we could do to save them.

Leaving the work to our men, Warrant Officer Kaneko and I went into the conning tower to meet the sub's skipper, a young lieutenant commander. The interior of the sub had a charged atmosphere, buzzing with excitement as the crew worked energetically unloading the cargo. These men were real sailors, different from us fish-out-of-water men on Buka enduring air raids day after day. The way they went about their work with both care and energy made me appreciate being on a ship again.

As I was discussing the next shipment with the skipper, the air attack alarm suddenly reverberated through the sub. The skipper abruptly broke off our conversation, shouted, "prepare to dive!" and left us both standing there. An uncanny tension and commotion followed. The sailors stopped unloading immediately, leaving the cargo on deck, and commenced an all-out effort to get the sub submerged as quickly as possible. In all this commotion, no one noticed Warrant Officer Kaneko and me.

My mind was a jumble of thoughts. With air raids a daily occurrence and an enemy landing imminent, there was no longer any logistics or transport work to be done on Buka. Staying on the sub meant going back to Rabaul where Fleet Command had a garrison. If I went to Rabaul,

I'd be saved. What's more, I had the perfect excuse, "the sub went into a rapid dive while I was on board at a meeting." For several moments, these thoughts flashed rapidly through my mind.

Warrant Officer Kaneko whispered, "Sir, let's stay here and go to Rabaul." Kaneko was a conscripted NCO over 40 years old with a wife and children back home. If the idea had occurred to me, he certainly had every reason to think of it. But I instinctively responded, "What are you talking about? Let's get out of here." For whatever reason—a young officer's pride, revulsion at his anticipating the despicable thoughts going through my own mind—hearing him say just what I was thinking really got to me.

There was nothing to do now but go. We exited the conning tower and, as if they had been waiting for us to leave, the hatch at our feet slammed shut with a forlorn clank. Once on deck, I was surprised to see that flares dropped by enemy fighters had lit up the sky as bright as midday. The sky seemed to be aglitter with countless firework explosions. The fighters circled menacingly overhead, occasionally dropping bombs. They seemed to be after Airfield No. 1.

The boats had cut their lines to the sub to avoid being pulled under and were now quite far off. They couldn't start their engines because their wake could be easily detected under the light of the flares and instead continued drifting farther away. Warrant Officer Kaneko and I stood stranded on top of the sub's conning tower with only 10 seconds or so before it would submerge. With the sky as bright as afternoon, I could still clearly see the submarine between the waves as well as the topography of the surrounding islands from my vantage point on the conning tower. Yet as the enemy fighters circled menacingly overhead dropping a steady stream of flares, they still didn't seem to know we were here.

The sound of both submarines and boats dropped

to a barely audible murmur, and beside the sound of waves and the explosion of bombs, I stood surrounded in frozen silence. In a few more seconds the sub would start to submerge. What were we going to do? For a brief instant, I stood upright in the conning tower. I really regretted that we hadn't stayed below, but now we had to stay focused on saving ourselves.

Just then, one of the boats off the stern of the sub engaged its engine and plunged toward us. It was Warrant Officer Uchida's boat. He had seen my silhouette when I stood up in the conning tower and was coming to rescue us. He gunned his boat's engine despite the marauding enemy fighters circling above. I slid down the conning tower and dashed all out for the stern of the sub. I sprinted full speed, dodging the bags of rice still lying on the sub's slippery deck. As Uchida's boat came up behind the sub, I kept running at full clip and leaped into the air. I grabbed the boat's gunwale but my legs fell into the water. Using all his strength, Uchida pulled me out. The thrashing waves had already moved the boat away from the sub, and I saw Kaneko on the sub's stern with a bewildered look. The boat was now 10 meters away from the sub. I shouted out to him; there wasn't a moment left to spare.

With a swishing sound and the swirl of foamy whitecaps, the sub began to submerge. As I screamed at Kaneko to jump, he leaped into the water and began swimming desperately toward us. It would be the end of him if he got caught in the whirlpool left behind by the submerging submarine. Just as we held out a stick to pull Kaneko in, the sub disappeared under the water and a whirlpool of water swirled out toward us. We were saved.

I would never be able to thank Uchida enough for what he did. He commanded his boat with true energy and skill.

Unfortunately, other than medicines, the cargo contained only one day of food supplies. A week later, another submarine shipment was sent, but Allied aircraft attacked the sub resulting in an aborted mission. Kawanishi commented, "We would never receive a second shipment from Rabaul, and as we neared the last of our resources, a decisive confrontation with starvation drew ever nearer."

It presented a huge problem. With no help on the way from outside, the Japanese military at Buka turned to farming, planting sweet potato and pumpkin in bombed out areas. "We didn't pursue this work with the zeal of sailors doing our duty, we did it to stay alive." They worked the fields, dawn to dusk, despite weak, under-nourished bodies. The work was difficult; coral clay stuck to their shovels and "growing sweet potatoes in this soil required constant and careful monitoring from the moment of planting".

Often after finishing work in the fields, Kawanishi would sit with Captain Ikeda on the veranda outside the officer's room. He describes one evening with Ikeda:

After incessantly complaining about the lack of food Ikeda would go back inside. It seems that he had brought some food with him when he came here from Buin. Without letting anyone in, he'd have a subordinate cook for him inside the room. He was an old man and this seemed to be his only pleasure. He seemed to think about nothing but food and going home.

I enjoyed watching the sunset from the veranda. As twilight descended, the leaves of the taro-like poison yam plants that abounded in the area stopped fluttering in the wind and quietly settled down. I still had some of the sake and canned rations that Chief Paymaster Yamada sometimes sent me, and I got them out. Despite the food shortage, we still had some of these sorts of things. As I fanned the hundreds of tiny insects attracted by the odor of the sake, my thoughts turned to home.

It was painful thinking of home. I would probably never see home again. Sometimes, when I thought about never going back, my heart grew heavy with sadness. I heard somebody singing a popular song about hunting rabbits in the mountains and fishing in the streams back home. Even when I hear that melody today, I become overwhelmed with emotion.

Soldiers, sailors and laborers—everybody knew this song. And when they sang, they sang while choking back tears. Grown men, their hair grown long and unkempt, belted out this song with tears flowing down their cheeks. Around this time, our food provisions had only just started to dwindle and the horror of starvation had yet to appear. We still shared the all-too-human yearning for home. Now the road home for everyone here had become the battlefield. In the evening twilight among the palm groves, I could hear singing from the labor troops' barracks, men marooned while on their way home yet desperately wanting to live.

With my emotions freed by the sake, I too sang, letting the gloominess work its way down to the bottom of my soul. Day turned to night. After writing a report for 8th Fleet headquarters under the flame of a handmade oil lamp, there was nothing left to do but go to sleep on my cot. Day after uneventful day went by in this way.

Chicago, 1945.

Chapter XVIII

BROKEN LEG AND CONVALESCENCE

THE SCOTCH EPISODE

March 14, 1944, Florida Is., Solomons

My Darling,

I received my orders today for return to the States. So it shouldn't be many days after you get this letter that I'll be phoning you from San Francisco. I've been expecting my orders for the past three weeks, but I didn't want to say anything about it until I had actually received them and knew positively I was going back.

I'm coming back on convalescent leave. Just a month ago, during some rough weather at sea, I was thrown off the bridge to the gun deck and broke my left leg, my ankle and my foot. The doctors said I'll be absolutely OK in about three months (two months from now). CDR Smith was nice about it. He had said that as long as I'll be going back home anyway within two or three months for leave and assignment to new duty, I might as well go home now and have my family look after me. So he recommended, and the Admiral approved, that I be returned to the US for convalescent leave and reassignment. It took three weeks for the orders to come through, and then I received them today.

161

My leg is coming along OK so it's nothing to worry about. I was flat on my back for three weeks—and boy, did the time drag—but I can move around a little on crutches.

They had to reset the ankle a couple of weeks ago, but the last X-rays last week showed perfect settings and everything is fine, according to the doctors.

Although my orders authorize air transportation, I'm coming back by boat, as it'll be more comfortable, and I can bring all my luggage and gear right with me so it won't get lost. I'm taking one of my ships over to Guadalcanal tomorrow to see Nick and to find out what ships are here that are returning directly to the US in the next few days. With any luck I should sail by the end of the week, March 18-29, and should reach San Francisco around April 5-8.

Of course, I'll have to report to the hospital when I get to Frisco, but it may take several days for them to make up their minds that I don't have to sit in a hospital and to arrange for me to join you in Los Angeles until my leg is well. The doctors here say I have another month (from now) with the cast and crutches, and then about a month more with a cane, before I'll be ready for active duty again. So, that should give me four or five weeks with you. I can hardly believe it.

I love you, Darling, and am already counting the hours until I see you. Love to Diane and Mary Fran. Worlds of love.

Vernon

—⚓—

March 20, 1944, Guadalcanal

My Sweetheart,

Have finally secured transportation on a cargo vessel, which leaves in the morning. We should arrive San Francisco in 21 days, which should make it about April 11.

It's a merchant marine ship and not built for passengers, but I think I'll be reasonably comfortable. I'm sharing a cabin with the navy lieutenant in command of the armed guard crew. The cabin on the main deck has its own head (bathroom) and is right next to the wardroom.

Two of our ex-LCI L skippers are going with me, Lieutenants Washer and Taylor, returning for new ships. We three are the only passengers aboard. They'll be good company.

When I arrive I want to go right to a hotel and get a room before I report to the commandant, so I can live there until they give me leave to go to Los Angeles. If this letter reaches you before I arrive, will you reserve me a room at the St. Francis, and leave word there where I can phone you? Could you meet me there?

This hardly seems real—that I'm coming home and will see you soon. Love to my girls. Loads of love to you.

Vernon

CONVALESCENT LEAVE

Jannotta spent a hectic but glorious month in Chicago after brief stays in San Francisco and Los Angeles with Navy doctors. It had been almost two years since his induction into the Navy; this break offered a chance to catch up with personal matters. Still hobbling about on a cane, he spent most of the leave at his Chicago home. A steady flow of people came to see him: family and friends, but also his accountant and former business associates. May, a decorator by profession, had worked intensively to get their new home ready for Vernon's homecoming. Situated on Chicago's near north side in a spacious double ceiling apartment with three bedrooms plus a maid's quarters, it was a stunning setting for Vernon to receive people. And he didn't disappoint. Relaxed, gregarious and full of "sea stories" he held forth.

During this period, Jannotta was in touch with his Navy assignment officer at the Pentagon. He learned two things. First, he would be given command of a flotilla of 36 LCIs scheduled to participate in MacArthur's Philippine Island landings. Second, with the assignment came a promotion to commander, great news that gave his leave an added element of pleasure.

Towards the end of his furlough, May put together a small dinner party. It included his brother Joe and wife Ramona, and Bob and Erna Zeddies. Bob was an old friend who at one point had lived with the Jannottas during a difficult economic period for the Zeddies, but subsequently had gone on to own and operate a successful candy bar distributorship. During Vernon's first combat tour, Bob kept him well supplied with Baby Ruths and other candy bars. It was like tapping into his own rich vein of ore especially when Spam was at times the only food available in the Solomons. But no Spam that night. Despite rationing, May had pulled strings to get a standing rib roast of beef and served it along with mashed potatoes, green beans and an apple pie dessert: all favorites of Vernon. And, of course, lots of scotch before and with dinner. The conversations were lively.

Following dinner, the men retired to Jannotta's study where Vernon had saved a high-end scotch. As Vernon was pouring the drinks, his brother Joe stopped to read a newly-framed Navy citation near the desk.

"Good lord! Vernon, this is something," exclaimed his brother who proceeded to read the entire Bronze Star citation, which ended with, " 'His outstanding initiative, leadership, and devotion to duty throughout the entire voyage and bombing attack were in keeping with the highest traditions of the United States Naval Service.' And it's signed by none other than Admiral William F. Halsey himself. Very impressive!"

In May 1944, Admiral Halsey was a national hero, a gutsy, get-the-job-done fighter whom the American public adored. The nickname "Bull" was affixed when Halsey made a series of raids in early 1942 against Japanese-held islands, and did it when their fleet was superior in operational capability to the US. He was no prude either; after his carrier pilots had flown an exhausting series of combat missions, he ordered the flight surgeon to provide whisky for the aviators.

Joe went on, "What was it like to serve under him?"

Vernon handed out the scotches and sat down in a large leather chair swirling his drink. "To start, let me say he's one helluva Naval officer who has done an outstanding job in the South Pacific. I was fortunate to serve under him. That said, I did get called on the carpet by him." Jannotta took his first sip and commented, "Interestingly, my run in with Halsey had something to do with scotch."

Eyeing his drink, he recounted the day he left Galveston. Jannotta had carefully stowed a supply of scotch—carefully, because it is against Navy regulations to store or drink liquor on a Navy ship. While he appreciated the ban, in certain situations he ignored it. In port at the end of the day, he would break out a bottle and enjoy an hour of relaxation with his officers or, upon re-entering port after combat, he would tuck a bottle or two under his arm and pay the harbormaster an official call regarding the berthing, repair and resupply of his ships. To show his appreciation, he would leave the scotch. Not surprisingly, Jannotta's ships were often declared ready for combat sooner than normally expected.

However, the combination of happy hours and gifting exhausted his supply. As a remedy, he issued orders stretching his authority and ordered a petty officer, fortified with a .45 caliber sidearm, to fly to San Francisco to pick up 30 cases of scotch. Given wartime shortages, it wasn't easy to pull off. All went well, largely due to the petty officer offering a bottle here and there during the return voyage. Unfortunately, Admiral Halsey's staff got wind of the affair and Jannotta was ordered to report to the Admiral.

When Jannotta was ushered into the office, he was nervous and stopped at full attention in front of the Admiral's desk. Out from under two bushy eyebrows, the Admiral glared at him.

"Lieutenant Commander Jannotta, I understand you issued special orders to fly a petty officer to San Francisco. Given the difficulty of moving men and supplies 9,000 miles to the South Pacific, I issue priority air travel orders only in extreme emergency. Furthermore, I understand there were personal aspects regarding your orders. Is that true?"

"Yes, sir," I said.

"Jannotta, your actions were absolutely out of line! Do you understand?"

"Yes, sir."

"Don't do it again."

"Yes, sir!"*

"I was lucky, no court-martial," laughed Jannotta, "only a slap on the wrist." Then, Jannotta raised his glass in a salute. "To Admiral Halsey," and emptied the last of his scotch.

*This episode was related to the author by Jannotta in February 1951. Logistics: moving men and supplies 6,000 to 9,000 miles was the Navy's greatest challenge in 1942 and early 1943, a lesson that neither WWI nor the peace time Navy taught. This issue had to have been on the mind of Admiral Halsey when he chastised Jannotta. Indeed, he was "lucky".

Buka natives were the first to reap the harvest of sweet potatoes from Japanese gardens. The natives are washing the potatoes in preparation for cooking, May, 1945. *Australian War Memorial*

Chapter XIX
THE SWEET POTATO THIEF

BUKA ISLAND

By late January 1944, the Allies had established three airfields in and around Torokina, Bougainville—one bomber and two fighter stripes. In order to neutralize Buka there were air attacks in December and January. It caused the Japanese forces to anticipate and prepare for an enemy landing that never occurred. Rather, Allied Forces moved north past Bougainville (and Rabaul) with amphibious landings on the western ends of New Britain, Green Island and New Ireland. Now the Japanese stranded on Bougainville faced a different enemy—starvation.

Kawanishi wrote that they ate anything that would fill their stomachs—lizards, field mice, snakes, hermit crabs—and when they exhausted these supplies, they turned to insects; they pulled off the wings of beetles, for instance, and cooked them. If it moved, they ate it. At the same time, they feverishly planted and tended fields of sweet potatoes. Kawanishi wrote:

> It was now March 1944. We watched the relentless rain of despair. Day by day, death drew nearer. When the first two or three men died from malnutrition, the dam burst and the death rate shot up. Those near death tried to hold out as long as they could, but one by one they expended their last breath. A man who had just tended the fields during the day might die later that night.

Our fields were the difference between nourishment and death. We had to keep going, and gradually we increased the area under cultivation. We tended our crops with everything we had. Every square meter equaled just so many human lives. I really don't know what kept us going. Impending annihilation terrified us. The daily scouring of the fields for food wore down our will to live. From March through May, countless died. The days remaining between us and starvation were hell on earth. What could be more horrible than our writhing in this hellish nightmare?

In the jungle, we had a sick ward covered by a leaky thatched roof with no enclosure and no partition filled with the dying. Really, it was just beds about 3 centimeters thick spread over a floor of skinny palm tree trunks. The black and red knots of the trunks were rough and hard, the blankets tattered and threadbare. When those knots dug into a skin-and-bones body, the pain was agonizing. Thin tatami mats, a little more than 3 square meters in size, were spread over the top of the palm trunk floor. The sick would be put upon them in twos and threes to sleep. Completely wrapped in their filthy blankets, strewn around the floor like a bunch of old rags, they looked like little piles of dirt. Sometimes these withered lumps of humanity—so withered I wondered if they were ever human at all—would manage to stir, sometimes stagger to the latrine.

The sun never penetrated to the jungle floor, but hot, wet air would seep in after about 0900 in the morning and fill the sick ward with its oppressive presence. Even in normal times, such heat is intolerable, yet the sick would wriggle around on the floor with their blankets clutched tightly around them. Even the barest glance of the malnutrition and malaria-ravaged bodies dying near them was a horrific sight. The hair on their heads was as pale and thin as the hair of a newborn infant. It seemed impossible that their skin, pale and as coarse as a

170

roughhewn wall, had blood coursing beneath it. They had
bulging hollow eyes. They unconsciously moved their arms.
Their blankets were filthy with the bile characteristic of
malnutrition, while the legs that stuck out from under
them were bloated from dropsy. Every one of the sick had
the face of an old man. Every cell in their body was dying.

Someone might say, "now, you hang in there, you'll
be well soon," and the dying man would raise his aggrieved
face and reply, "okay, okay," like a babbling child. Their
spirits were dying along with their bodies. Already, their
most human emotions—morality, a fighting spirit—were
gone. So, too, were reason and fear. They had been reduced
to a child-like state, driven by animal instinct alone. And,
in time, they would drift away into the final sleep of death.

One day in March the rains broke, and Kawanishi decided to
visit another unit. There was a communal field on the way, a few acres
in size, where the Japanese carefully cultivated a crop of sweet potatoes.
The field had four caretakers, older non-commissioned officers, many
of whom were farmers in civilian life. Their role was to oversee the
plantings and guard against theft. It took sweet potatoes from four-and-
a-half to five-and-a-half months to reach maturity. Potatoes sprouted
in their third month and then grew very quickly. At this moment,
the field had potatoes about the size of a person's big toe. Kawanishi
expected the Japanese to run out of food in two months and the fields
represented a "last ditch effort to survive. Plundering the crop now
would only mean starvation two months later." Kawanishi insisted on
the most severe punishment for individuals caught stealing.

On this particular trip, Kawanishi, along with several fellow
officers, made the excursion at night and as they hurried along the path
in the pitch black jungle, using torches made from palm husks to lead
their way, they came to a field.

I noticed a dark shadow squatting amid the field greenery.
A sweet potato thief! Instinctively, and without a word, I
charged into the field. My officers followed. The furrows in

171

this field were big, and even in the excitement of pursuit, they weren't easy to get over. Tendrils caught my foot, making running difficult. Two, maybe three times, I fell, but I kept after that dark shape. The thief too fell several times as he fled.

I had closed in to about 10 meters when, in resignation perhaps, the thief collapsed and made no attempt to get up. Laying there with his head thrust between the sweet potato leaves, he gasped so violently that he seemed on the verge of death. I too breathed heavily, but it only fueled my rage. "Get up!" I shouted. The fellow just lay there gasping for dear life. The others caught up. The field sentry, gun at the ready, also appeared. The sentry jumped in front of me, grabbed him by the collar, and pulled him up to his feet. Like a child throwing a tantrum, he slumped down on the furrow with his back to us, guarding his face with his hands.

We could see him clearly now in the moonlight. He wore tattered laborer's clothes and had a filthy handkerchief wrapped around his neck. I saw malnutrition immediately: The blistered face, dull expression, stringy hair, and blackened fingers. One hand jerked feebly in the moonlight as if to block a blow. The other hand tightly clutched to his chest a sack with a few kilograms of sweet potatoes inside. His eyes were wide with terror at the prospect of being beaten yet he held on to the potatoes for all he was worth. My rage yielded to the pathetic sight of this withered, emaciated fellow.

"Son of a bitch!" the sentry shouted as he tried to pull the fellow up. But it was no good. Instead, like a stubborn child, he remained curled up between the furrows clutching his sack. Even then, he tried to put the raw big-toe sized potatoes, freshly dug and still covered in dirt, into his mouth. He was not going to give up those potatoes for anything. Finally, the sentry pulled him up and grabbed the sack away from him. As if in a trance, the fellow

snatched a skinny little potato and tried to put it in his mouth. This let loose a volley of punches and kicks. He collapsed screaming in agony. But he still wouldn't let go of that potato. Under the soft white light of the moon, I stood dumbfounded at the wretched sight of his repulsive, twisted, mud-caked face, his discolored mouth still gnawing on the potato even as he was pulled to his feet. How pitiful and hopeless it all was. I felt completely defeated. I passed the night in the caretaker's hut. As I walked across the sweet potato field in the cool breeze the next morning, I couldn't get the sight of that miserable fellow out of my mind. When I went to the infirmary a few days later he was already just another corpse.

The potato thief episode was but one example of a mounting crisis that came close to overwhelming the Japanese on Buka. The fields the Japanese worked so hard in tilling only provided food for 3,000 of their 7,000 in number. Before the crisis passed, some 4,000 Japanese soldiers and support staff died of starvation and disease. In reaction, the starving Japanese soldiers often stole food from the native villagers, inflicting violence along the way. The conflict set up a dynamic for change.

It was a dynamic on which Kawanishi would capitalize.

With Hitotsubashi University judo team. Kawanishi is kneeling, second from right, holding "Boston Bag".

Chapter XX
WINNING HEARTS AND MINDS

Kawanishi, having grown up in a culture that typically views non-Japanese populations such as the Koreans "as members of an inferior race", his attempts to bridge the cultural differences between the natives and Japanese were highly unusual.

Creating a climate of cooperation between the islanders and his own countrymen presented a problem of figuring out what patterns animated the islanders' culture. It was a puzzle that intensely concerned him. He observed:

> *Since the Japanese army invaded Bougainville, the islanders' attitude toward us had gradually changed. At first, they enthusiastically greeted us as their liberators from the yoke of white domination and they treated us with respect. Over time, however, they began to keep a cautious distance, and since the American landing (at Empress Bay), their attitude had subtly but perceptibly changed.*
>
> *Besides the lack of food, trouble between military personnel and the islanders occurred constantly. We could control the situation while we had military goods to trade with the islanders, but once these were gone, personnel steadily encroached upon their fields, and some even abducted women and committed murder. The Japanese soldier came to be seen as cruel and heartless, a savage and dangerous animal. Because of this violence, the islanders came to see us as the enemy.*

To address the growing problem, Kawanishi commenced "studying the circumstances in which the islanders lived" with the goal of reducing the violence on Buka. He described Buka as a small island extending 30 kilometers north to south and 8 kilometers east to west, separated from Bougainville to the south by the narrow Buka Passage. It had been settled several hundred years ago by two native peoples; one group from New Caledonia populated the coastal areas and subsisted on fishing, while the other group came from Papua, New Guinea, penetrated inland to the mountains and practiced agriculture. Currently, the two groups lived together amicably, gathering once a month to trade.

Initially, the islanders and the Japanese co-existed peacefully. But when the US landed at Empress Bay, the bitter fighting and constant air attacks disrupted the lives of the islanders. The exposed villages along the coast were shelled, palm groves were bombed—even agricultural fields were targeted by warplanes. The coastal tribes retreated into caves along the coral reefs while the mountain tribes abandoned their fields and built new villages deep in the jungle. The fighting drove them from their homes and sources of food.

Kawanishi noted that these conditions gravely affected the islanders' hierarchical village structure. A survival-of-the-fittest mentality took hold. As the village chiefs lost their fields, and with it their power and prestige, the villages, now split apart and difficult to control, responded only to brute strength. The village structure began to collapse—even the family unit was threatened.

Philosopher Bruno Bettelheim described violence as the behavior of someone incapable of imagining other solutions to a tumultuous problem. The turning point in breaking these patterns, like the one facing the Buka natives and the Japanese military, requires a 180 degree turn away from violence and to imagining a creative act that explores "the heart of on-the-ground realities where violence has dominated human affairs".

Kawanishi devised a plan. It began when he ignored Japanese prejudices and scorn for non-Japanese people and reached out to the Buka natives in a caring, thoughtful manner deploying what are called "soft skills". His actions required a creative visioning that moved him to pursue a goal toward what is fine and away from violence. As a start he studied the cultural patterns of the islanders' lives and summarized his findings:

The islanders had an extremely strong sense of attachment to things. Everyone knew who owned a particular sweet potato or piece of fruit, and taking such a thing was a grave transgression. Even taking a coconut from someplace in the middle of the jungle without permission was a crime; only the owner could grant permission. This was why the islanders could survive with a minimum of physical effort. They didn't horde things for the purpose of exchanging them later for something else, so even in the jungle with its abundant resources, a person took something only when they really needed it. Fields and fruit trees were the islanders' storehouse, their most precious asset. The destruction and scarcity wrought by the war on the islanders' natural environment made these resources all the more indispensable to them. Women were assets, too. The islanders valued a wedding dowry to be at least four pigs along with two seashell necklaces and two palm trees. Willfully violating these customs was an unthinkable insult, yet the Japanese military ignored them.

There was no telling what chaos lay ahead if we continued to ignore this situation. So what measures could we take to avoid serious conflict with the islanders?

As I pondered this problem, I recalled a class on British Colonial policy I had attended at Hitotsubashi University taught by a Professor Yoichi Itagaki. It was just a university course whose content held little direct application to the real world, but if it were to ever come in handy as a last resort, this was it. With my recollections of the class as a guide, I racked my brain for several days.

Out of Kawanishi's musings came a plan.

First, select 20 non-commissioned officers (NCOs) to train and dispatch to all the villages. These islander relations personnel would wear military attire to project an image of proud soldiers. They would assist village chiefs in rebuilding their hierarchical organization.

Second, provide winter and foul weather NCO caps and clothing, normally worn on ships at sea but now lying unused in storage, to village chiefs in recognition of their status and as a symbol of their authority.

Third, teach the islanders Japanese farming methods. The crops from fields used to teach farming would be split 50-50 between them and us. Since they could use fields employing Japanese farming methods indefinitely, give them to the chiefs as their personal possessions.

Fourth, show them how to harvest salt and distribute the yield the same way as with crops.

Fifth, use vehicle parts and oil drums to teach them blacksmith techniques for making spades and fighting swords, and let them keep whatever is made.

Sixth, show them how to fish with canned explosives and how to preserve the catch.

Seventh, create a school in the jungle to teach these things, attended by about 10 percent of the islanders at any one time. Everyone brings a one-week supply of food, and after a week, the group leaves while a new one comes in. During this time, the islanders are put through group drill training for deployment as rear echelon personnel during times of fighting.

As a first step, Kawanishi sought permission of the 8th Fleet through the Japanese 87th Garrison Commander, who strutted his authority "like a self-important schoolboy", but who came up with no objections. Preoccupied with the need of food for his troops, he really didn't care about the natives, nor did he see them as part of the problem. If they were truly in his way he could turn to force. All this worked to Kawanishi's benefit.

In practice, the plan did turn out to be ingenious. The school that Kawanishi set up and ran at Telatu was a huge success and they saw results within a month: the villagers calmed down, the chiefs reasserted their authority and looked impressive in their hats, and the number of tilled fields steadily increased. The islanders seemed truly happy. The non-commissioned officers sent to the villages conducted themselves splendidly. Theft by Japanese soldiers ceased, and conflict along with it. Potatoes and fish were gathered in abundance. Everyone was satisfied.

In June 1944, Lieutenant Kawanishi went with an army adjutant to meet with Isa, one of the four big chiefs on Buka Island.

Kawanishi had learned that Isa wanted to give him a gift. The chief was eager to express his gratitude because Kawanishi had restored, even enhanced, his agricultural lands, the source of his wealth and power. He assumed the gift would be fruit or something similar. Instead, Isa presented him with a ceremonious gift that stunned him and the army adjutant who accompanied Kawanishi.

"The captain is still young. Please accept this gift," said the chief. A girl stood with a shy expression next to a palm-leaf basket equipped with two handles for carrying. She was perhaps 17 or 18 and of breathtaking beauty.

"I repay my debt of gratitude with this daughter, who also has consented to go stay with the captain," said the chief. "A meeting of village elders deliberated this matter, and the village-leaving ceremony was already performed this morning. If you were to just take a woman without giving anything for her, in violation of our customs, then we would take revenge. But this time everything has been done according to custom so you have nothing to worry about."

Whenever Kawanishi glanced at her, she would smile broadly in return. It left him with feelings of confusion.

Months earlier, the entire population of Buka—natives and Japanese alike—had been in mortal struggle against starvation and each other. Now they had become friends, almost family. A mutual respect had formed to the point where a prominent chief was presenting his

179

daughter as a gift of gratitude to Kawanishi, the man who was largely responsible for this transformation.

In October, during a time of limited air attacks, Kawanishi and several officers made a tour of the island to check on their program and continue to build good relations with the islanders. The non-commissioned officers in the villages were informed in advance so that they could prepare.

They arrived at one village at mealtime. Provisions for a feast had been set out including delicacies like roast sloth and wild pig, taro, bananas, papaya, and coconut. According to custom, the elders feasted first, followed by the chiefs and, finally, by the rest of the village.

"We ate to our hearts' content," wrote Kawanishi.

After the meal, the villagers gathered with Kawanishi to voice complaints and to ask him questions. He found the islanders civilized, and no different from a rural Japanese village. "The only difference was the color of their skin."

A court was held to deal with the case of a young widow who was upsetting the village's "standards of morality by enticing their youth with her loose behavior". It offered an example of how the natives ran their day-to-day lives. In this instance, Kawanishi was informed that an appropriate punishment would be to have her stand in the village square naked from dawn to dusk "as a warning to others".

The next day, the chief solemnly handed down the punishment. To Kawanishi's astonishment, the widow, "with seemingly bold resolve, whisked off the red *laplap* wrapped around her waist, raised both hands above her head, and opened her stance by about a step so that her body formed an X." Never having seen a stark-naked woman in such a posture, Kawanishi was "absolutely stupefied".

Villagers gathered around her, mainly young men and squatting children, chins in hands. She survived the morning reasonably well, but when the noon heat hit, flies started coming around. The flies on Buka are quite big, aggressive—more like horseflies—and swarmed around her groin. The woman jerked her body to send them scattering, but they were relentless, lighting upon her again and again, as spectators jeered. "It was obvious that this was the worst sort of a punishment for a woman," wrote Kawanishi.

During his time on Buka, Kawanishi went through a metamorphosis; at first, he couldn't tell the black-skinned islanders apart. "It was as if they were covered with black paint." But as Kawanishi interacted with them, he gradually noticed differences—the lips, or the skin on the palm of the hand or the bottom of the feet revealed dark brown skin as often as black. He found some islanders "magnificently handsome with the statuesque nose and even the porcelain-like skin of a Greek sculpture, while others reminded me of a gorilla". Both men and women had frizzy hair that "sat piled atop their head much like the hair on the head of the Buddha". Also, at first "their bodies stank intolerably of palm oil and sweat, but in time I came not to notice it in the least. It was all very fascinating."

So when Chief Isa presented Kawanishi with his beautiful, smiling daughter, it was a conflicted moment, but Kawanishi knew he couldn't possibly accept. Finally, he told it to the chief straight.

"I truly appreciate your kindness, but I simply cannot accept your daughter."

The chief was thoroughly dejected. "We've already performed the ceremony for her leaving the village. Now she cannot return."

I broke out into a cold sweat as the half-sobbing girl was taken away.

Despite Kawanishi's refusal of marriage to Chief Isa's daughter, his plan to work with the natives was a success—primarily because he defied Japanese military culture and "walked a mile" in the shoes of Isa and the islanders. It took a special kind of courage to do so. In University of Chicago Professor Jonathan Lear's book, *Radical Hope*, the story of cultural devastation that faced the Crow Nation in the late 19th century defines courage. It is based on Aristotle's thought that courage is a virtue which lies between a deficiency (cowardice) and an excess (rash boldness). There are five criteria:

1. A courageous person has a proper orientation toward what is shameful and what is fearful.

2. Courage aims toward what is fine.

3. A courageous person must grasp the situation that he or she is in and, through experience, exercise good judgment.

4. Courage paradigmatically involves the risk of serious loss and of enduring certain pains.

5. Bold acts that derive merely from optimism are not themselves courageous.

Clearly, Kawanishi's work with the Buka natives came from genuine courage.

Probably neither the Japanese nor the natives would have survived the food crisis alone. On the contrary, they could well have entered a very destructive mode. Instead, Kawanishi was able to overcome the grimmest situation by first forging a compassionate approach to working with them. As a result, the implementation of his plan transformed Japanese interactions with the islanders who, "without hesitation, wholeheartedly lived together with us as one".

Kawanishi's dealings with the Buka natives give us a new perspective on him as a leader, one worth examining more closely. His actions put in place a series of changes that alter the natives' interactions with the Japanese military. Most leadership can be described as transactional or operational. For instance, Jannotta and Kawanishi received orders daily and were superb leaders in carrying out their duties. They responded to events, rather than offering event-making decisions in their work.

In James McGregor Burns' book, *Transforming Leadership*, he describes an "event-making" leadership style that can be termed transformational. President Lincoln produced a transformational event during his second administration by freeing the slaves. It changed society in a fundamental manner.

At a lesser level, Kawanishi's work in bringing peace between the Buka natives and Japanese military shows him as a transformational leader.

His efforts required an understanding of the natives' (adversaries') culture; his decisions also required good judgment. Kawanishi had the ability to look down range, make clear and logical decisions, and understand the effects of his strategic judgments and strategies.

To achieve his goals, Kawanishi conceived a seemingly simple model made up of four elements:

First, a genuine humanistic approach to dealing with the natives as friends, as opposed to adversaries.

Second, the ability to step outside one's own culture and to understand an enemy's way of life.

Third, problem definition. In Kawanishi's case, lack of food and resulting starvation caused the Japanese soldiers to steal from the Buka natives and to commit rape and murder. Also, in the resulting chaos, chiefs lost supervisory control of their villages to opportunistic Japanese soldiers who manipulated village affairs to their advantage.

Fourth, courage, given the problem, to design and implement a creative but realistic plan that doesn't turn to violence as a solution.

How Kawanishi effected this remarkable change from an island in warfare and crisis to one of cooperation is a compelling story of leadership in the Pacific War.

General Douglas MacArthur wades ashore during initial landings at Leyte, Philippine Islands, October, 1944. *US Army*

Chapter XXI
"I SHALL RETURN"

While Kawanishi struggled to survive on isolated Buka, the Allies pressed ahead to the Philippines. In May 1944, as stipulated, Jannotta was promoted and given command of a flotilla of 48 LCIs. By July, he was on his way back to the South Pacific to join Vice Admiral Thomas Kinkaid, Commander 7th Fleet as part of General Douglas MacArthur's Allied Forces' scheduled offensive in the Philippine Islands.

MacArthur's strategy to recapture "Leyte and then Luzon" was agreed to by President Roosevelt and Admiral Nimitz in July 1944. However, Admiral King preferred to leap-frog the Philippine Island of Luzon, where 260,000 Japanese troops were concentrated, and land on Formosa, a step closer to the ultimate goal of Honshu, the main Japanese Island.

The US Joint Chiefs of Staff debated the strategy; Vice Admiral Raymond Spruance and Rear Admiral Forrest Sherman (both of Nimitz's staff) argued persuasively that hitting Luzon, followed with landings at Iwo Jima and Okinawa, was a more sensible approach to Honshu. In the end, King agreed.

Interestingly, President Roosevelt supported MacArthur, partly, it has been speculated, to end any chance of MacArthur running for president in the 1944 elections. There were also the practical considerations of whether enough troops were available for landings at the alternative target, Formosa, Admiral King's objective.

BATTLE OF LEYTE GULF
October 23-26, 1944

In August 1944, Admiral Toyoda's chief of staff stated that the Imperial Japanese Navy "must make a desperate effort to defeat the enemy" and stop its unrelenting movement toward the Japanese Islands. When it did challenge the US fleets in the Battle of Leyte Gulf on October 23-26, 1944, it became the largest naval battle ever fought. The word "desperate" describes the Japanese efforts; Imperial Japanese Naval forces were divided into three operating units.

First, a northern group off Cape Engano under Admiral Jisaburō Ozawa consisting of one fleet carrier, three light carriers (with only 109 aircraft versus the typical 250), three light cruisers, and nine destroyers represented the sacrificial bait to draw Admiral Halsey's 3rd Fleet north, leaving the Leyte landing beaches unguarded. Indeed the ruse worked. Halsey took the bait, attacked it and destroyed the minimally armed and manned northern force.

Second was a force that included two battleships, two heavy cruisers, a light cruiser, and destroyers under Vice Admirals Nishimura and Shima (two independent battle units) with orders to steam up the Surigao Strait, south and east of the Leyte landings. Their goal was also to draw US Navy surface ships away from the landing area. Opposing the Japanese ships was an overwhelming US Navy force made up of 6 battleships, 3 heavy cruisers, 2 light cruisers, 28 destroyers, and 45 motor torpedo boats under Rear Admiral Jesse B. Oldendorf.

The resulting action culminated in a decisive US victory. In the end only five destroyers and one heavy cruiser remained afloat of the original Japanese striking force. No US Navy ships were lost.

The third unit was a substantial central group under Admiral Takeo Kurita, encompassing 5 battleships, 10 heavy cruisers, 2 light cruisers and 15 destroyers whose primary role was to attack the Leyte beaches and put the Allied landings at risk. Hence when Admiral Kurita entered Samar off the Leyte beaches, unprotected by Halsey's Task Force, he only found 16 slow and lightly armored escort aircraft carriers (Taffy 1, 2 and 3 with 450 aircraft) and a handful of destroyers. Yet they made life hot, and Kurita, not knowing that Halsey was north, assumed he was facing the 3rd Fleet carriers. After sinking a light carrier (CVE) and three destroyers, he retired from the battle. Poor command structure and faulty communication hampered both sides.

"Our defeat at Leyte," said the Japanese navy minister, Admiral Yonai after the war "was tantamount to the loss of the Philippines and the end of our resources."

Preparations For Luzon Landings
A Special Task Force

In a letter dated December 18, 1944, Jannotta told his wife that Captain McDowell, when ordered by Washington to set up a task group for a specific mission, had asked for Jannotta and his LCIs. "I didn't know what it was all about until I met Captain George Mentz (Commanding Officer of Jannotta's Task Force) and he told me it had all started weeks ago with and through Captain McDowell.

Two hundred and sixty miles separated the landing areas from Leyte to Luzon, where the US had its air bases. In contrast, the Japanese had 70 airfields on the islands with an estimated 400 aircraft, many of which were concentrated around Manila. MacArthur's landings at Lingayen required combat air support for his fleet in transit as well as for troops on the beaches. And distance precluded fighter support from the US airfields at Leyte.

To solve the problem, MacArthur elected to land on the lightly defended island of Mindoro, south of and adjacent to Luzon, to establish an airfield at its main city, San Jose. The action bypassed many enemy-held islands and placed air support for the Lingayen offensive close at hand. US Navy historian Samuel Eliot Morison called it one of the "boldest" moves of the Pacific War. Timetables for the Philippine offensive were tight: October 20, Leyte landings; December 15, hit San Jose, Mindoro beaches; and on January 9, 1945, land at Lingayen, Luzon. As a supplement to the landings at San Jose, a special Task Force 77.11 was formed. It had two assignments. The first was to bring material for the fighters at the newly constructed airfield at San Jose—aviation gas, torpedoes, bombs, ammunition, spare parts, and more troops—on December 30 (D-day plus 15). The second was to rig Jannotta's 23 LCIs with steel beams extending the height of the ships by 10 to 15 feet in early January. When underway, the modified LCIs might register on Japanese radar as capital ships such as cruisers, and, in the accompaniment of 30 PT boats, be interpreted as an invasion fleet, and drawing Japanese troops away from Lingayen south to Batangas Bay, Luzon.

USS LCI L 624
December 25, 1944, Leyte, Philippine Islands

My Darling,

Merry Christmas! I hope all of you had a happy one. I will be anxious to hear all about it and about everyone.

This hasn't been much of a Christmas for our men. We've been moving around and up forward so much that Christmas mail hasn't had a chance to catch up with us. So, very few Christmas packages have been received. I did manage to get turkeys for all ships yesterday, so we had a turkey dinner. Yesterday afternoon I sent around unofficial word that all ships could break out what little beer they had left and serve it on board as a part of Christmas Eve celebration. We had eight cases left on our ship for the 80 men and officers I carry with me, and we planned a party for the men and arranged for the officers to spend the evening together in the wardroom. I had my three group commanders who are present come aboard, also.

We sat down to our first bottle and relaxation just after dark. Jim Marshall (my operations officer) had received one package, which he had not opened, so he opened that and we shared in inspecting the numerous small gifts it contained. I had a fruitcake from Auntie Blanche—others had nuts and candies. We were just getting comfortable and enjoyably relaxed when General Quarters sounded and everyone had to grab helmets and life jackets and get to battle stations. The Japs were raiding us again. Lots of flak—a large number of bombs dropped—one plane was caught in the searchlights and the first shot from a 40 mm on a ship astern of us hit it—burst it into flame and it trailed down to the water, with the trace streams of flak following it all the way down. It was a lucky hit. It's very seldom we get a plane at night. The action lasted about 40 minutes before "all clear" came over the radio.

I left the conn, went down to the ward room—the other officers drifted in—we got settled, and then the alarm howled again. It went that way all night, up to 0200. We had six raids. After the third we gave it up—there wasn't any Christmas Eve spirit left in anyone.

I've been writing this in between conferences, studying of charts and operation orders, and General Quarters so far. They started as usual tonight, just after dusk, as I said. I hope to get over to some other ship staying here, in the morning, to see if they have mail for me.

We hit Mindoro first—them jump off from there. Will probably be out of touch with ships going back, on which we could send mail, for two to four weeks. Don't worry, Darling, if you don't hear from me for a little while.

Give my love to our three girls, to Nickie, Nick, Mother, and all the family. Loads of love to you, my Darling.

Vernon

KAMIKAZES!

USS LCI L 624
January 4, 1945, Mindoro, Philippine Islands

My Darling Girl,

I had thought to write you every day—but I just couldn't. Every moment has been filled with suspense, action and emergency that I haven't been able to sit down and collect my thoughts for even a short moment.

We have been under attack—air—continuously now for nine days. It has seemed months. Day and night, we've had no let-up. The men and officers are all in from time strain of being at battle stations anywhere from 5 to 20 times every 24 hours for periods of a half hour to two or three hours—of fighting planes off—of watching helplessly while they blow up some other ship, which might just as well have been yours. No one's had any sleep, only in snatches, at the guns, on the deck, in the conn. And, in between, the frantic effort to save men's lives—pulling them out of the water, transferring them to our ships that have surgical teams on them for emergency treatment, then the worst to the beach to the army hospitals; trying to save ships; fighting fire, if they are not sunk.

From Leyte to Mindoro we advanced under heavy escort with a large number of other ships—with my LCIs and PTs of our task group, there were about 90 all told. They started hitting us our first night out. Not in big numbers, but a few at a time, so they could get through our thin air coverage—and continuously, through the night, through the day, etc. My ships were all lucky. We were not hit—although my ship had one torpedo not only pass under us, but actually graze the bottom—another six inches of draft and we'd have been blown up. They got four large ships right out of the middle of our convoy. My LCIs did all the rescue work—pulled about 190 survivors out. There were no survivors from one ship—only two on another.

The day we landed, after the rest of the ships and escort unloaded and started back, they started again on us. That afternoon, the 30th, they got our command ship and tender. Mine was lying about 150 yards the other side of it as the Jap plane dove in—and my other 22 LCIs all around. We put up a terrific fight, hit him, but couldn't stop him, and he came right on through. This new tactic of theirs—"Suicide Divers" (kamikazes) is really horrible. A plane dropping bombs, or diving at you to throw a bomb or a torpedo, gives your ship a chance—he will miss more times than he will hit. But, when instead of that he simply aims his plane at you, and flies the plane itself right into you with his bomb load, he never misses. He got the *Orestes*, and we lost most of our command staff on it: Captain Mentz, our Task Group Commander, Commander Kramer (Chief of Staff), LCDR Jones, and several other officers.

So, as I was third senior officer in the task group, and both seniors to me were casualties, I have taken over command of the Task Group 77.11. My staff is sadly depleted. We lost all our supplies, reserve ammunition, and gas for the PTs. None to spare in the area, and none coming up before we are scheduled to make our first attack. All our task group records were lost, much of the planning arrangements, etc., were made personally by Captain Mentz, and I did not know the details. It has been very difficult picking up the loose threads, putting them together and completing the operational plans and orders. The job of working out details with army and air has in itself been a long and tedious job. They have so many commitments and problems, too, but they have been fine and are giving me most of the help and support (air) I must have.

My plans are completed—ships (LCIs) and patrol boats (PTs) are all ready—what they have left. We leave this afternoon for our first strike. I'm writing this at 0530 this morning.

I did not want to tell you any of this, Darling, because I did not want to upset or frighten you. I hope somehow it will not. But I'm so filled with it, I can't do anything else.

I've been very lucky so far (those of us who are OK all have). The men are wonderful—they may be all in, but their spirit is superb. I've had to evacuate a few whose nerves cracked—my staff engineering officer is one of them (he fought it, but when it gets you, you can't help it)—and I feel his loss keenly, too.*

I think our luck will continue. I hope so. There's every chance we can pull this attack off and get away with it. There is one thing certain—my Task Group is surely going to give the Jap some jitters and headaches (in its diversionary "assault" at Batangas Bay) for a few hours that we hope will materially upset some of his plans on Luzon for opposing our main landings.

I don't know whether they have been releasing information on this new weapon of the Japs (the suicide bomber), or of our losses. Probably not. So don't talk about it. I don't know why it is, but I had to. But remember, although the Japs have been getting many of our ships this way—because it is sure fire and never misses—in the over-all picture it's still a small percentage of what we take in against him. The going may be tough, but there is no question that we're making good progress and will eventually beat him.

I want you to know, Sweetheart, I love you. You have been and are all the life holds for me. You have given me more of happiness than most men could have ever believed possible. Oh, there's so much I wish I could express to you—of our life, our love, our happiness together. It's 1900 and I must go.

Give my girls and Nicky a kiss for me.
My love to Mother. Worlds of love to you, my Darling.

---

*Commander Jannotta "keenly" cared for his engineering officer, Dewey F. Barich. He encouraged his full recovery by correspondence and via telephone. Their relationship flourished. In civilian life, Barich was named president of the Detroit Institute of Technology in 1958. As a testament of their relationship Barich dedicated a professorial chair in honor of Jannotta.

For his actions in saving the command ship, *Orestes*, Jannotta was awarded the Navy Cross; and for succeeding to the command of Task Force 77.11 and carrying out its mission under the most difficult circumstances, he received the Silver Star.

Jannotta's letter home dispenses with the kamikaze hit on the *Orestes* in just a sentence. Details of his actions surfaced years later. It was the summer of 1956. Lieutenant Junior Grade Ned Jannotta, Vernon Jannotta's nephew, was flying a US Navy AD-2 propeller-driven fighter/bomber as part of the Navy's 6th Fleet operations in the Mediterranean. The Cold War was in one of its hot periods. As a matter of routine, Soviet submarines tailed and spied on the fleet's movements and occasionally a Soviet military aircraft flew provocative feints at the fleet. Not surprisingly, an air of tension surrounded the Navy's operations. It was in this context that Lieutenant Junior Grade Jannotta and 23 squadron mates assembled in their carrier's ready room for a highly sensitive flight briefing. The mission involved a tricky and dangerous flight maneuver that simulated the delivery of "A–Bombs" to Soviet-controlled cities. To do the briefing, the 6th Fleet Admiral sent his Chief of Staff, Captain N. Burt Davis, USN, a Pacific War veteran. To a carrier pilot, especially to a Lieutenant Junior Grade, a captain is very senior rank and is accorded the utmost respect. So when Davis ducked his head through the hatch to enter the ready room, which is typically full of self-confident pilot banter like the locker room of a successful football team, there was an uncharacteristic hush.

The Chief of Staff began, "Who is LTJG Jannotta?"
All eyes turned to Ned who raised a tentative hand, "I am, sir."
"Any relation to Vernon Jannotta?"
"Yes sir. Nephew."
"Bravest man I've ever known."

Following the briefing, Captain Davis pulled Lieutenant Junior Grade Jannotta aside to tell him the story of his relationship with Vernon Jannotta when the two men had served in the Philippines on Task Force 77.11.

Davis said the Task Force, made up of 100 ships and crafts—

destroyers, liberty ships, LSTs that included Jannotta's 23 LCIs and 30 PT boats which Davis commanded—left the base at Leyte and during the 3 days en route (December 27-30, 1944) were under attack night and day—a total of 31 times—by kamikazes and dive bombers. Seven ships were sunk or destroyed en route. It was a period laden with action and tension and the ships' crews catching catnaps while at battle stations.

On arriving at San Jose Bay, Mindoro, on December 30, the air attacks continued as they discharged Army troops and unloaded equipment. In the early afternoon, four kamikazes were seen lazily circling the fleet at high altitude—seemingly detached observers. Suddenly they nosed their aircraft over into suicide dives. All hell broke loose as every ship opened fire on the kamikazes, but to little effect. Three ships were hit, one of them was the LST *Orestes*, the command ship, loaded with 60,000 gallons of aviation gas and 50 tons of explosives, including 160 torpedoes. Struck amid-ship, it immediately burst into flame, the explosion blowing many officers and men into the sea. The order was given to abandon ship. With men swimming everywhere, Jannotta immediately got his LCI underway to pick up survivors.

A major drama began to unfold. With the *Orestes* all but engulfed in flames, Jannotta pulled his LCI alongside, drew his 45-caliber pistol and, pointing it in the air, asked for volunteers to put out the fire. Then, in the midst of exploding ammunition, smoke and fumes, he led a fire-fighting contingent on board the *Orestes*.

On the way to Mindoro, Davis had seen a sister ship to *Orestes* take a hit by a kamikaze. The monster explosion turned that ship and its men into mist. Only a few empty life jackets were found. With this memory in mind, Davis said, he was riveted by Jannotta's fire fighting. In fact, the whole fleet was. It continued for four and a half hours. In that time, two of Jannotta's party were killed by small arms fire and another had his nerves crack. Finally, they wrestled the fire under control. Jannotta emerged from inside the ship, jumped up on a stanchion, and proceeded to relieve himself on a small remaining fire; a man well endowed, Jannotta's theatrics added to the drama. Task Force bullhorns blared in celebration.

Though Vernon never boasted of it, Davis was not the only man to recognize Jannotta's accomplishments in the Philippines. From December 30, 1944 to February 2, 1945, Jannotta acted as the Commanding Officer of Task Force 77.11, reporting to Brigadier General W.C. Dunckel of the US 8th Army. His primary responsibility was to support Dunckel's air and ground operations in the area of San Jose, Mindoro. In a commendation letter about Jannotta to Admiral T.C. Kinkaid of the 7th Fleet, the general wrote:

> Commander Jannotta commanded a task force in the Mindoro operation in a superior manner in addition to planning operations of this force. Commander Jannotta gave me willing and outstanding efficient service in the transportation of troop units and seizure of areas on Mindoro and the Island of Marinduque. Commander Jannotta's fearless, prompt, and superior leadership in rendering aid to US vessels that had been struck by enemy bombs resulted in an appreciable saving of lives of personnel and government material.
>
> In commending Commander Jannotta, I am heartily supported by all members of the air and ground forces in Mindoro, and it is our belief that he is one of the most outstanding Naval officers with whom we have served.

This commendation, in addition to a Navy Cross and a Silver Star, demonstrated Jannotta's skills in planning and executing a most difficult mission. It is a profound example of the Navy's operational capability at the mid-organizational levels, a strength that was critical to winning the war.

Leyte, 1945.

Chapter XXII
REST AND RECUPERATION

WAR UPDATE

On December 13, 1944, Vernon Jannotta turned 49, just 15 years short of the then-expected American male's life span. To his men, who were mostly in their teens and twenties, he was an anomaly: he could out-work and out-drink them and remain lucid and functional even under the most trying combat conditions. Packaged in a small, wiry body he seemed to defy normal male physiology. Truth be known, he was gifted with a constitution that contained huge energy reserves; as a hands-on leader who prided himself in directing the operations of his 48 LCIs, often without sleep, he needed these reserves.

But even with this wonderful asset, the intensity of battle conditions in 1944 and early 1945 were beginning to take a toll.

In early February 1945, Jannotta and his flotilla were back relaxing in Mindoro. For the first time in two weeks, yet what seemed like months, he was not under pressure.

He had completed his mission as Commanding Officer for Task Force 77.11, a command he assumed when the kamikaze attack on the *Orestes* had wounded or killed the Task Force staff. Importantly, Jannotta had the satisfaction of knowing his Task Force had done a good job. Four admirals called him from their flagships to tell him so. The finest commendation, though, was from Admiral Kinkaid (Commander 7th Fleet—his immediate boss on this job) with his simple but welcome, "Congratulations on a fine job done, Commander Jannotta."

Jannotta speculated that his Task Force would be dissolved shortly and his LCI flotilla sent back to the Commander, 7th Amphibious Force, at Leyte. As to the future, he wrote, "I don't believe there'll be any more major operations by 7th Fleet for a while, but we have much back-tracking to do, in clearing up Japs in spots and islands we've bypassed." Indeed, now that Manila, Luzon was secured, Jannotta and his LCIs were headed back down the Philippines, first to retake key Mindanao ports and from there to landings in the oil-rich Dutch East Indies. As to his homecoming, Jannotta wrote to his wife:

If I can stick it out another seven months, which would make my current combat tour of 14 months out here, I think I can get home—that would make 14 months out of the States on this second tour of combat duty, and that seems fairly established as a policy out here now. And it surely seems to me, I will have done my share by that time, and you, too, my sweetheart.

Sweetheart, I'm no good at writing. My mind races with a million things I'd like to tell you, but they just will not translate through my fingers. Maybe tomorrow I can do better. I love you, dearest girl, very, very much.

Iwo Jima

While Jannotta recuperated at Leyte, Allied Forces were occupying and securing the majority of Luzon. This victory raised the question of where to invade next. In a conference in San Francisco on January 20, Admirals King, Nimitz and Spruance agreed that the final two steps before invading Japan would be landings at either Iwo Jima or Chichi Jima (the Bonin Islands), followed by the invasion of Okinawa. On February 19, Marine Expeditionary Troops under Lieutenant General Holland M. Smith did land troops on Iwo Jima.

The Japanese, under Lieutenant General Tadamichi Kuribayashi, had "transformed the central island into a fortress", honeycombing it with tunnels connecting bunkers and other defensive structures.

More than 21,000 Japanese troops were committed to defending it, in their words, to a "desperate battle"; surrender was not an option. The US committed 30,000 Marines or a total of 40,000 men including Navy supplemental forces. Despite horrendous Allied, Naval and air bombardment, dislodging the Japanese required close-in attacks using flame-throwers and US Marine demolition devices. In the end, the Marines suffered 24,701 casualties including 5,610 dead—casualties greater than incurred on D-Day in France. Of the approximate 21,000 Japanese troops, only 216 were captured.

OKINAWA

The final step before invading mainland Japan was Okinawa, an island 80 miles long and on average 8 miles wide. Geographically convenient, it lies 340 miles from mainland Japan and 830 miles from Tokyo Bay, and was judged an appropriate air and naval base from which to launch the invasion of Japan.

Emperor Meiji had formally annexed it in 1879 when it was rumored that the Okinawans might appeal for US protection during a scheduled visit to the island by President Ulysses S. Grant. Underdeveloped and rural, its population in 1940 was 800,000 and was made up of mixed blood: Chinese, Malayan and Ainu. Most of them were farmers living in thatched huts or small frame houses subsisting on "tiny fields in which were raised barley, sugar cane, beets, cabbages, and sweet potatoes". Anticipating the Allied invasion, Japanese military assigned the 32nd Army made up of 67,000 soldiers and 9,000 Imperial Navy men to meet the Allied onslaught. To supplement their forces, the Japanese conscripted 39,000 Okinawans who were assigned rear-militia duties. The senior officer for these forces was Lieutenant General Mitsuru Ushijima, who was located in the south of the island, where the Japanese defensive positions were particularly foreboding. Also, as a part of the defense were 2,000 to 3,000 aircraft, of which at least half were kamikazes, all prepared to attack Allied shipping around Okinawa; and they didn't disappoint. During the three months of fighting, they accounted for 30 US Naval ships sunk, 368 ships and craft damaged and 9,724 personnel casualties including more than 5,700 dead.

On April 1, the Allies began landing 102,000 Army and 81,000 Marine Corps personnel under the banner of the 10th Army, Lieutenant General Simon Bolivar Buckner, Jr., commanding. They found little opposition. The Japanese strategy was to draw the Allied troops into narrow valleys where air and sea power were less effective. Like Iwo Jima, these valleys were honeycombed with tunnels that hid Japanese troops and their weaponry. Okinawa, like Iwo Jima, took a terrific human toll.

William Manchester was a distinguished biographer, novelist, historian, and not least, a marine sergeant with the 29th Regiment of the 6th Division at Okinawa. In his memoir, *Goodbye Darkness*, he wrote what it was like to be on the ground at Okinawa in the Spring of 1945.

"By sheer chance, I had chosen a spot from which the entire battlefield was visible. It was hideous, and it was also strangely familiar, resembling, I then realized, photographs of 1914-1918. This, I thought, is what Verdun and Passchendaele must have looked like. Two great armies, squatting opposite one another in mud and smoke, were locked together in unimaginable agony. There was no room for flanking operation; the Pacific Ocean lay to the east and the East China Sea to the west—I lingered on in that hammock, repelled and bewitched. It was a moonscape, hills, ridges, and cliffs that rose and fell along the front like grey stumps of rotting teeth. There was nothing green left; artillery had denuded and scarred every inch of ground. Tiny flares glowed and disappeared, shrapnel burst with bluish white puffs. Jets of flamethrowers flickered here and there stirred up the rubble."

On April 1, Manchester's regiment put ashore 3,514 men. By the end of July 1945, 2,812 had fallen. In the midst of the madness, he ticked off his lost buddies: Lefty, Chet, Swifty, Bubba, Barr, Horst,

Pip, and Mo, most of them college students. Last, he recalled Shiloh Davidson III, Williams College '44, who on a twilight patrol was eviscerated by an enemy mortar, thrown on to a "wire and lay there illuminated by green enemy flares, screaming for his mother, until he died at 4:30 a.m." For Manchester, "Death had become a kind of epidemic."

Many of these deaths took place on Sugar Loaf where Manchester and his regiment fought. According to *Newsweek*, it was "the most critical local battle of the war", resulting in 7,547 Marine casualties. The human toll at Okinawa was horrendous: US casualties were 50,000, 12,000 of whom were killed; 107,000 Japanese perished in combat, an additional 20,000 died due to entrapment in caves. Only 7,400, who were captured, survived. By best US estimates 154,000 Okinawans died. These numbers total 231,000 casualties. Winston Churchill called the battle for Okinawa "among the most intense and famous in military history". Others might term it barbaric man at his worst.

US Marines gathered in front of a Japanese dugout on Bougainville, January 1944. *AP Photo*

Chapter XXIII

BACKTRACKING

In an early 1945 letter to his wife, Jannotta proclaimed that his command—45 ships (3 were lost), 200 officers and 1,263 men—was "the best goddamn flotilla in the whole Pacific". He went on to proudly state that he was the only officer with a command of four groups (12 ships per group) versus the standard three, and the only reserve officer commanding a flotilla. At the close, he asked forgiveness for his "crass bragging".

In the spring and summer of 1945, the 7th Fleet, including his flotilla, were clearing Japanese from the southern Philippine Islands and the oil rich Dutch East Indies, which had previously been bypassed. Their initial target was Zamboanga at the tip of the southwest peninsula of the Philippine Island of Mindanao.

Jannotta called it "the most carefully planned and conducted and executed amphibious operation" he'd ever seen. It consisted of 33 of Jannotta's LCIs and 4 large transports (APA) to carry the troops; 18 landing ships, medium-sized ones containing artillery; and 24 LSTs, loaded with tanks, trucks and service troops. The landing area, a quarter of a mile wide, was approached between coral reefs and rocks at the beach line. Two hours prior to landing, a cruiser and destroyers drenched the area with salvos while mine sweepers cleared the approaches to the beaches. Then followed the LCI gunboats and rocket ships which laid a barrage on the beach targeting Japanese gun positions. And just before the APAs and the LCIs reached the beach, three flights of B-24s performed precise bombings of an adjacent airfield. The LCIs hit the beaches in three waves, 15 minutes apart—the waves went in line abreast, made the beaches right on time, disembarked the troops in four minutes or less, retracted and retired at full speed, keeping out of the way of the incoming waves. Casualties were light, only six, recorded Jannotta, who went on to comment on a beaching incident:

> Not a single LCI was hung up on a reef, and all 33, but one, were able to make a dry landing—that is, put the troops right on shore without even getting their feet wet.
>
> The only LCI that didn't make a dry landing had a headquarters company aboard, including 22 officers and a general, instead of the usual six or seven officers of a troop combat company as on the other ships; and this ship hit the shoal part of the beach about 50 yards off the shore, so the general and his officers had to wade ashore about neck deep in water, which proves that the Navy plays no favorites, and amused the "Dogfaces" greatly.

At dusk on March 11, Jannotta departed Zamboanga with 14 of his LCIs and 18 other ships (LSTs, minesweepers and destroyers) bound for Leyte with orders to prepare for the next operation by the 20th. It left Jannotta with a very tight schedule to complete repairs such as engine overhauls, fuel up and take on water and provisions.

USS LCI L 624
March 14, 1945, Leyte, Philippine Islands

My Sweetheart,
Working against time, as usual. Arrived here late afternoon of the 13th and have to sail at dawn on the 19th, and, in between, get my 33 LCIs ready that will go with me on this next operation.
Here's just a small segment of what's on a flotilla commander's mind.
As I approached Leyte the afternoon of the 13th, I started calling (by radio) certain of my ships that should

have been in Leyte (SP Harbor) to see if: (a) spare parts which we had had on order for all ships for weeks and were supposed to be in Leyte by this time, had arrived; (b) 40mm guns which com 7th Phib had finally approved for me to mount on each ship, and which were overdue, had arrived; (c) where the hell my disbursing officer was whom I hadn't seen or heard of since I had flown him down to Humboldt, New Guinea, three weeks before to locate some things that we had ordered from the States for the flotilla in October, and which had been sitting in Humboldt for a month; (d) whether they had any mail waiting for us, or if it had been sent to Mindoro; (e) whether a crippled ship I had left in Mindoro with request to 7th Phib to send to Leyte for repairs, had yet arrived, etc., etc. I found the air full of chatter from "foreign" ships, which we soon identified from their code calls as 3rd Fleet LCIs. The harbor was apparently lousy with them and they were all hollering for repair facilities, provisions, etc.,—everything I wanted. That meant we'd have a merry time of it, trying to get the services we needed in the short time allotted.

So, instead of taking my ships into anchorage for the night, I detached them all and sent them to a watering place in Samar which I was fairly sure the 3rd Fleet ships wouldn't have found out about as yet, with orders to get fresh water to capacity before morning, and then to proceed to anchorage for repairs. I put a full speed and beat it for the Tacloban area to find com 7th Phib Forces flagship to hear what it was all about and to get priorities on dockings and repairs.

As I came in visual signaling distance, she started sending me messages—"Report to Operations for Orders," etc. Got aboard her just before dark taking my operations officer, my engineering officer, my communications officer, with me. Operations then gave me my orders: I was directed to report to Admiral Fechtler with 33 of my flotilla's 45 LCIs.

To complicate Jannotta's planning, nobody knew much about the operation (called V-5) and he had only 17 of the 33 LCIs he needed. Furthermore, the troops for V-5 were at Humboldt, which meant leaving Leyte a day early.

In the end, Jannotta lined up 26 ships of his flotilla which were scattered from Mindoro to Subic Bay, Luzon to Zamboanga, and got another seven assigned from another flotilla to make up the 33. By quick thinking, politicking, and calling in favors from friends, Jannotta got his ships serviced and provisioned ahead of his competitors from 3rd Fleet.

At daylight the next morning, Jannotta set his flagship alongside the senior repair tender, and in an hour had a definite time schedule of docks, with the tenders and ships allocated and fully worked out. Then he proceeded to the anchorage area he had assigned his ships. He found all but two had completed watering overnight and were in anchorage, and that the other two were scheduled to be ready at 1000 hours. He brought two group commanders on board and gave them the schedule of work to be accomplished for all ships including docking, repairs, fueling, fresh provisions, engine and machinery check, and tune-ups, radio check, and repairs. Because of the intense preparations, there was no liberty for any ship. But according to Jannotta, "things are pretty well under control and moving along now".

> I'm praying there are some letters from you in this mail that's gone to Mindoro and that it'll get back here before we shove off. I want to know you are all right, and of everything you're doing. I'll try to write again before we sail.

One of the operations, Tarakan, was the first of the amphibious operations in a new area—the Netherlands East Indies—to be staged under Admiral Royal, using Australian troops.

Just before his ships were ready to shove off in late April 1945, he received an invitation to a dinner party from the Admiral. There were about 90 officers at the party with dinner, music, entertainment, and refreshments.

The Admiral and all his staff were invited, including the unit commanders of the task groups such as Jannotta, and also the brigadiers and general of the Australian Army and even the commander in chief of the Australian Forces. Jannotta explained:

"You see, this is the first offensive operation in which the Australians are participating out here in a major way, so we have all the bigwigs with us. They are all grand chaps—big fellows—good fighters—regular men that Americans take to and like. The division we are taking on this first Borneo job is the one that finally stopped the Germans at Alamein in Africa.

"We had a wonderful dinner (where these admirals dig up these swell steaks I have never been able to figure out) in grand company, with a dandy band (the Admiral's), and all the various drinks one could possibly desire."

—⁓—

While preparing for the next offense Jannotta found time to relax.

A couple of nights ago, a bunch of the war correspondents, etc., who are going with us on this operation asked me to come over and have dinner with them on the LCI 635 and then play poker. I think I told you we have about 40 with us—Australians, Hollanders, Americans—Navy and Army public relations officers with them to look after them and censor their dispatches. Had a most entertaining and enjoyable evening listening to their stories of experiences on other fronts and in other operations. Then we played poker—seven of us. An Australian Navy commander, an Army captain (from MacArthur's GHQ), an Aussie correspondent, a Canadian correspondent representing Dutch papers, a Dutch Navy lieutenant commander, an American correspondent, and myself. The cards were against me, and I lost for three or four hours straight, then my luck changed and I couldn't be beaten. I ended with almost everything they had, in the damnedest assortment of American dollars, Philippine pesos, Dutch guilders, and Australian pounds you ever saw. It took my paymaster some time to figure it out and exchange it for American dollars for me.

Well, my Sweetheart, I'll have to sign off. My thoughts are with you constantly. Love to our girls and all the family. Loads of love to you.

Jannotta's mission (Tarakan, Borneo) was a success; in fact Admiral Thomas C. Kinkaid, Commander 7th Fleet, awarded Jannotta a Bronze Star. "For meritorious conduct as commander of the LCI Transport Unit of Task Force 78.1 during operations against the enemy of Zamboanga, Philippine Islands, and Tarakan, Borneo, from March 6 to May 5, 1945. Commander Jannotta displayed exceptional administrative ability in the executive of assault and resupply missions. His skill and leadership under combat conditions were material contributions in the success of the amphibious campaigns. His conduct throughout has distinguished him among those performing duties of the same character."

—⁓—

The pre-invasion levity stood in contrast to the fight itself. After the battle of Tarakan, Jannotta described it in a letter.

During the landings we had some mortar fire and had torpedoes launched at us from shore—a new one to us. One passed my ship about 400 yards off the port side. Another passed across the stern of the nearby LST and hit another ship but did not explode. When they do explode, it's curtains.

This was the toughest landing condition we've ever had. Mines, underwater obstacles (three rows of them—steel rails set in the bottom, sticking up), a very shallow beach gradient with a bottom of about 5 feet of mud that no man or machine could get through, and an 11-foot tide that, when it went out (twice a day), left an impassable mud stretch several hundred yards off shore. The minesweepers did a wonderful job cleaning up mines for us—we only lost one ship to a mine. The demolition teams did a heroic job blasting gaps through the obstacles, but the goddamn mud and tide made it tough. We couldn't get the ships in, unloaded and out on the same tide. I had one hung up for 18 hours on the beach—right smack in the area where a Jap mortar battery was letting them fall. All afternoon and all night they exploded all around the ship, astern and both sides, but not one hit the ship directly. I had all men keep off the topsides and remain below decks—it was all that could be done, except pray. The ship was shredded with shrapnel holes but, believe it or not, not a single man was hurt. Another miracle. Others weren't so fortunate.

This place is a great oil center so, of course, as the oil storage tanks were shelled or bombed, they set up huge fires with great columns of heavy black smoke. The buildings and huts in villages and towns burned with white smoke. It always hurts me to see the towns with buildings and huts get shelled and bombed and burned, but, of course, the Japs build their defenses through these and fill them with snipers, so they must go. The natives, most of them, have cleared out by the time we start. The Japs here shot all of them—every single male native—in the foot so they couldn't work for us, as they retreated.

I had to be on the conn practically all the time for three days—orders coming and going by radio constantly. The heat from sun and humidity was simply terrific. I've been in many hot places in the past two years out here, but nothing ever compared with that at Tarakan.

By spring 1945 Jannotta began to feel the strain of combat and the constant pressure of operations:

I have had what seems like months of very rugged duty and

action—I think I have a good case of insomnia. Haven't slept for the last four months except in snatches. Now, when I can get some sleep, I go to bed and never close my eyes until three or four in the morning and then, of course, they waken me a couple of hours later. I haven't used sleeping pills because I'm subject to call any time, and I'm fearful of them. I still take vitamin tablets daily. I swear I'd have folded up long ago if it weren't for them.

In a May letter, with his ability to function as a flotilla commander in question, Jannotta approached Admiral Royal.

May 18, 1945, Morotai

My Sweetheart,

I finally decided I'd lay my cards on the table to Admiral Royal and get his advice and help. I decided, too, I might as well go the whole route and ask not only for emergency leave, but for permanent detachment from this duty and reassignment to shore duty in US. The Admiral was really grand. He advised me to put my request in writing to Admiral Daniel E. Barbey—through himself. He said, in absence of Captain McGee, he himself would forward it, recommending approval. He said I would have to carry out these next two operations to which I have already been assigned, but felt sure I would be relieved and sent home, then. I've written the request, he has endorsed it recommending approval, and it's on the way. If it comes through, the date of the second operation now being July 10, maybe I can be relieved, on my way by the 20th, and home in early August. I still do not dare think of it too much but, Darling, I do think I stand a good chance.

As Captain Sugan—Admiral Royal's chief staff officer—put it, "He's all for you"—and that helps greatly, to have his support and favorable endorsement.

Love to all the family. Worlds of love to you.

May 25, 1945, Morotai

My Own Darling Girl,

It has never failed—or, rather you have never failed me. Always, just when I was shoving off on an operation, and might not have heard from you for several days, our very last delivery of mail before we sail brings a letter from you. Our mail just came aboard and there were two letters from you—nice long ones.

The other night the Admiral (Noble), who is in command of this operation since Admiral Royal's death at Brunei Bay (he died of a heart attack), and his staff gave a party at the officers' club for all unit commanders (Navy, Army, Air) on this operation. Liquor, food, music (by an Army band), women and dancing. Printed invitations (quite swanky), copy enclosed. The women (were made up of) Red Cross (about 8) and Aussie nurses (about 50). My supper and dancing partner was a Captain Mollie Milne, very friendly, good fun. It was a good party—and a welcome break in the monotony of work, war, heat, natives, men only, etc., etc.

Thank you, my Sweetheart, for the Father's Day message. I am not just counting the days until I start back home—I am literally counting the hours.

June 4, 1945, Leyte

My darling,

Today I received the enclosed copy of a dispatch (radio) sent by com. 7th Phib to Bureau of Personnel recommending leave and re-assignment to duty in US for me.

The Admiral acted on this without delay and by dispatch. So, it seems to me, it is practically assured I will get it. I'm positive the bureau will approve. It shouldn't take longer than four to six weeks to get a relief out here for me—that really seems too good to be true. But it certainly looks as though it's in the bag now.

Worlds of love.

NGELE NGELE ISLANDS
June 6, 1945

Jannotta was taking it easy. He had gotten permission from the Dutch authorities to land his 40 LCIs on a beautiful island called Ngele Ngele just a few miles from Morotai. The natives were friendly and unspoiled and he called it one of the finest beaches he had ever seen.

> For the first time since we left the States, the men can be ashore as much and as long as they want. The natives are busy making native craftwork, trading them for cigarettes, cloth, etc. The men are having a wonderful time trading, playing ball and pitching horseshoes on the beach, wandering over the island, swimming, fishing, aquaplaning (they've rigged boards towed by the ships' wherries with outboard motor for this), having beach parties (weenie roasts and beer), etc. I have two movie projectors with me, so we also show movies every night. The natives have built a picturesque and very practical palm hut (to our specifications) for officers' club and bar right on the beach.
>
> Me—I'm sleeping most of the time, and doing just as little paper work as possible.

Jannotta was exhausted. He noted that the next operation would be his last. And then speculated about his stateside duty alternatives:

> I do not know how much leave they will give me. I would

be entitled to thirty days—but I may get only two weeks. Whatever it is, that time will be ours, yours and mine— and whatever you want to do, or wherever you want to go, whether it's to Colorado, Minnesota, the moon—or just live quietly in Chicago. I have done my share of duty in this war—at sea, outside US, and in combat. You have borne your share of sacrifice and worry. I am willing to continue to give my services to the end of the war, only if (1) I can serve in the US where you can be with me, and (2) providing this is agreeable with you. If not, I will, when I get home, make immediate application for inactive duty—and I think I could get it approved. We'll talk this over and decide what we should do when I arrive.

So, my darling girl, it won't be long now. I love you with all my heart.

USS LCI L 624
July 4, 1945, At Sea

My Sweetheart,

Well, that's over, and we're on our way back to Morotai. We took Balikpapan, Borneo, the center of the most productive oil fields in the Dutch East Indies. You know, darling, in advance of any action, although I would fight against it, the thought would always creep in, "Well, I wonder if this is where I get mine." I guess everyone has to fight that idea off. On this operation, it seemed to be in my subconscious mind most of the time, though I tried very hard to push it out. It was to be my last combat operation— my last time in action. I had my orders back to US (received them the day we sailed for Balikpapan), and somehow that seemed to make my chances slimmer and the risks greater than ever before. Believe me, I prayed. Well, that's all over. Thank God, it is over and my last action is behind me.

Most officers think as I do—it will take another 12 to 14 months to whip Japan, and we won't be ready for our first major invasion for some time yet.

This is the 4th of July—a very different one from the 4th of two years ago, when we were just stopping the advance of the Jap, and beginning to take the offensive ourselves, but were working on a shoestring, and taking a beating in the air, on the sea, and on land. I was at Rendova, in the Solomons, with a task unit of LCIs and LSTs on the Munda, New Georgia, assault operation, and the Japs bombed the hell out of us. Had three of my ships hit badly—two sunk (later salvaged them), and I was peppered with shrapnel myself. Today, we are handing it out to the Japs and taking very little in return. It's a pleasure to see it, believe me.

Enough of that. I hope I'll never again have to write about "War".

The atomic bombings of the cities of Hiroshima and Nagasaki in Japan were conducted by the United States during the final stages of World War II in August 1945. *US Army*

Chapter XXIV
"The Last Embers Burned Out"

Twenty-five years separated Kotarō Kawanishi from Jannotta. Letters from loved ones, in the case of Jannotta, played a major factor in his morale, whereas Kawanishi never mentioned getting any letters. Towards the end of the war, he casually mentioned in his diaries that both his parents were dead, without referring to the circumstances or how he learned of their deaths; a stoicism surfaced that allowed Kawanishi (and likely many other Japanese combatants) to deal with adversity. At age 24, without wife and children or parents, he primarily expressed a longing for Japan (home) as a *place*, in contrast with Jannotta whose declarations were stated in human terms (wife, daughters, grandson, mother). The differences between the two men were part generational, part cultural.

Kawanishi's stoicism and a tenacious resolve surfaced as the Japanese forces faced superior enemy troops in a hopeless battle:

> *By the end of 1944, the food situation in the Buka zone, while still severe, had become manageable. It was around this time that we faced our next crisis.*
>
> *As the Americans turned their attack toward the central west Pacific in a drive to Iwo Jima and Okinawa, Bougainville was left isolated and abandoned. But this didn't mean that the fighting had ended for us; Australians had taken over from the Americans the task of mopping up the Japanese forces that remained on the island.*

In the Buka zone, personnel had been reduced to 2,700. Of these, only around 800 were combat able, including construction personnel pressed into frontline duty. But chronic malaria kept half of this number out of action at any one time. We also lacked ammunition, and our weapons consisted mostly of pistols and sub-machine guns in a number too few to go around. Most alarming of all, while we were preoccupied with growing food, humidity had reduced all our grenades and artillery shells to duds.

A critical factor in planning any military operation was the protection of the sweet potato fields the navy had planted. As Kawanishi wrote, "We couldn't very well hoist these fields onto our backs and transport them to the interior of the island." So the fields determined to a major degree where their troops fought. While the army held off the enemy, the navy worked to get themselves prepared for battle. They constructed defensive positions, built up food provisions, dried sweet potatoes to use as field rations, and also worked with the islanders on Buka to expand supplementary field plots. The Imperial Japanese Navy weapons consisted of two rapid-fire machine guns and two mountain artillery pieces, along with some field artillery, small arms and a few machine guns that the army had. Kawanishi wrote, "To make up for our lack of arms, we stripped down bicycles, equipment we couldn't use, and used the material to make bayonets and swords, removed gunpowder from aircraft bombs to put into artillery shell duds, and used construction crew detonators and fuses to make land mines. This is what we had to fight our well-equipped adversary." Unable to directly confront the Australian troops, they employed guerrilla warfare tactics. From January to late March, the Japanese held off the Australians. Dense jungle, mountainous terrain and coral reefs were natural allies:

We were not going to fight the whites on their terms; we would prevent them from using their standard tactic of concentrating overwhelming air and fire power on an open battlefield. We would make our stand in the jungle where locating targets was difficult and from there make the enemy fight for every piece of ground.

Construction personnel simply didn't have the training or physical strength for such close combat. But they could plant mines, so that's the kind of guerrilla warfare we used. Nor did we fight at night. A squad attacking at night risked losing their way and starving in the jungle.

Instead, a squad set out from its jungle base to infiltrate enemy territory while it was still light. Beneath the thick jungle canopy perpetual twilight reigned and the leaves, accumulated on its floor over thousands of years, muffled the sound of footsteps. By the time the squad drew near an enemy camp or supply depot, night had fallen.

In the morning, a blanket of fog settled over the jungle. Of course, the morning fog also settled over enemy camps. Away from the frontline, the enemy let their guard down, drinking late into the night and sleeping it off in the morning. While they slept, the squad feverishly planted mines under barracks and warehouses and then returned to the jungle's edge with their cords in hand. Just before sunrise, they exploded the mines and disappeared into the jungle.

The Australians, asleep in their barracks, would awake at once and rush outside. The camp would erupt into general pandemonium as squads of scouts plunged into the jungle wildly firing their weapons. But the jungle provided a thick shield, and their bullets did no more than ricochet ineffectually off the trees.

The jungle terrain defense rested on their digging of *takotsubo*. A *takotsubo* was a deep vertical hole generally dug beneath a large tree trunk or other object in order to protect it from heavy shelling. Each *takotsubo* could protect two or three men. The Japanese blanketed their *takotsubo* defensive perimeter with the mines that they had made from artillery shells. The mines were rigged to explode when a cord to which they were connected was pulled. The men in *takotsubo* exploded them when enemy scouts and patrols got close to their position. A camouflaged path used for bringing food provisions also served as the means of contact with the rear.

Their guerrilla squads consisted of up to five men who carried mines deep behind enemy lines to attack camps and supply lines. After making their attack, they wove through the jungle back to friendly territory.

Our initial attacks were mostly successful, but the enemy steadily became more vigilant and began to surround their bases with barbed wire.

Still, our guerrilla tactics seemed to have a psychological effect on the enemy. They became preoccupied with guarding their positions and their advance quickly lost momentum. It may be that we had become obsessed with fighting and nothing else. We knew, of course, that the outcome of our fight with the Australians would in no way affect the course of the war. But we couldn't leave the island either. Fighting was our only choice. As soldiers, we were taught that it is our duty to inflict as much damage as possible on the enemy, lighten the burden on the mainland, and, if necessary, die like Japanese. If we were rescued, even at this late date, we would have shown our countrymen that we had performed our duty.

Kawanishi continued:

We next targeted the enemy supply line to the front. The squads planted mines in the early morning and then lay in wait on the jungle edge. The first convoy of trucks passed through by nine o'clock. They pulled the cord when the middle of the column was right over it. This took out the guards with automatic weapons sitting on top of the trucks. By the time a patrol formed on the side of the road, the squad had already disappeared into the jungle.

The Australians were in effect fighting a phantom

army. They almost never saw a Japanese soldier. If they had ever managed to do so, they wouldn't have believed that this was the Japanese soldier inflicting so much harm on them.

Shirtless, barefoot, tattered pants, skin and bones—this soldier was just a tramp with a mine on his back and a machete in his hand.

The enemy slowly pushed the front line closer to the Japanese base, though the Japanese guerrillas launched constant counterattacks. Ten men, for example, using a dug-out canoe, paddled under cover of darkness across Buka Bay to camp on a small island adjacent to the Australian base. On the following night, they slipped into the enemy's harbor. The attack crew stealthily clambered up the sides of a landing craft and a large boat, planted the explosives, and lit the fuse which began slowly fizzling. The crew of the canoe furiously rowed off. After three minutes, a roar and flames erupted as the bombs exploded. Now engulfed in flames, the engines of the landing crafts exploded, the awesome sight of the flames reflecting off the water.

A second attack was launched several days later but due to poor coordination was unsuccessful. On a third attempt the canoe crew was ambushed and killed.

The enemy had thoroughly studied our tactics and it became increasingly difficult for us to wage guerrilla-style warfare. Attacking despite the low chance of success against the enemy's superior firepower brought an increasing number of battle deaths. One after another, skilled soldiers died in the field, including our battle-hardened guerrilla leader. The end was coming.

Daily air attacks, mortar shelling and bombardment from three destroyers and a light cruiser decimated the thinly armed Japanese forces hiding in the jungles. It seemed that in days they would be overrun. And to underscore their desperation, food supplies were dangerously low.

One evening during the crisis Kawanishi sat with his superior, Navy Captain Kato, briefing him on that day's operations. He recorded the meeting:

Over a cut-in-half oil drum with a dull light provided by the flame of palm bark to ward off mosquitoes, we discussed the situation. Wearing full-length khaki army fatigues and flight boots, the captain listened to my assessment, all the while nervously fanning himself from marauding mosquitoes. Kato had dressed this way ever since coming to Buka, both out of a sense of style and fear of malaria; he was probably the only one who never got it and no matter how hot it got, he wouldn't wear anything else.

Our conversations turned to home. The captain talked about his family in Sendai and other things. Then, after a brief silence, he said, "You don't want to die alone when the time comes. Go together with me. Really we have no choice but to die together. I want to die after helping you commit seppuku. *How about it?"*

The end came on August 14, 1945.

I was sleeping in the little room under the bluff that I shared with the chief paymaster when the captain sent for his subordinates. It was eleven o'clock in the evening. I dressed and went to the cave where the captain had his quarters. I assumed he wanted to discuss tomorrow morning's distribution of sweet potatoes harvested from the fields or preparations for the shift of operations to Buka. When I got to the cave, I saw the captain looking down at his desk, upon which a small oil lamp burned. It was unusual for Captain Kato to be up at this hour. He looked despondent.

Coming to his side, I said, "You asked for me, sir?"

Silently, he passed me a single page of a telegraph message. It said: "Suspend fighting at once. Secure the frontline. Burn all sensitive documents at once. Wait for further orders." It was a cable from Rabaul. I was speechless. Stunned, I discussed the cable with the captain. The fire of the oil lamp cast a reddish reflection on the rough, uneven walls of the cave. The reddish-light reflected on the captain's face.

"Sir, we've lost. Haven't we?"

"Yes, that's right."

"Does anyone else know about this, sir?

"Just the communications chief."

I said nothing. The captain said, "What shall we do?"

Again, I was silent. I remember feeling how all the overbearing strain that I had carried within me up to then suddenly seemed to drain from my body, leaving nothing but numbness behind. The reason that we had fought for four months was suddenly gone. I felt no joy at being saved; I didn't feel anything. All my emotions just melted away until there were no feelings left inside me.

"Sir, please send orders to all the troops. We should burn confidential documents right away."

As noted several nights earlier, the captain had suggested that he would help Kawanishi commit *seppuku* and together they would die. But there was no talk of this.

After a bit, Kawanishi got up and left the cave. The communications chief and Kawanishi set about burning confidential documents. "No miracle was going to save us; there was nothing else left to do," reflected Kawanishi. They placed a drum in front of the cave, poured some aircraft fuel into it, lit it on fire, and began tossing thick sheaf after thick sheaf of documents into the flames. The fire grew higher and higher, its flames reaching the top of the bluff. They watched the flames in silence. In twos and threes, the other officers gathered around.

I will never forget that fire and that night. The message was conveyed to everyone in the field. The biggest uproar occurred in the conscript barracks. The news was too

223

sudden and too momentous to digest. The unthinkable had
actually happened.

A single gunshot rang out. An orderly later reported
that a soldier scheduled to attack that night shot himself.
The captain ordered every soldier to maintain discipline.
My drifting thoughts stopped to wonder about what was
going through that man's head when he took his life. I
was so tired. I had no energy to do anything. I watched
the flames. I watched everything turn to ashes. I watched
until the last embers burned out. And then I just sat. It
was finished. It was all over.

What Kawanishi didn't know was that on August 6, 1945 a US
Army Air Force B-29, named the *Enola Gay*, dropped an atomic bomb
on Hiroshima—and what turned out to be a key war-ending event.
It occurred about the time Jannotta arrived in Chicago for his leave.
The *Chicago Daily Tribune* on August 7, 1945, read:

POWER OF THE UNIVERSE TAPPED TO CREATE
NEW MISSILE, Washington, DC, August 6—An
epochal announcement of a new secret weapon,
foreshadowing an early end to the war with Japan,
was made by President Truman. The weapon is an
atomic bomb, a projectile which looses the colossal
energy of an atom with an explosive force of greater
than 20,000 tons of TNT. The bomb described as
the greatest force in history, was said to pack a
punch equivalent to that delivered by 2,000 B-29
Super Forts. Moreover, the bomb was said to be
capable of making the United States invulnerable
to attack and to open the way to a revolution in the
production of energy for industry and transportation.

On August 9, a second bomb was dropped on Nagasaki and
the Soviet Union declared war on Japan. The Japanese surrendered as
reported by the *Chicago Daily Tribune*.

TRUMAN TO PROCLAIM V-J DAY AFTER EMISSARIES COMPLETE SIGNING OF FORMAL TERMS, Washington, DC, August 14. The war is over. President Truman at 6 o'clock tonight (Chicago time) announced the unconditional surrender of Japan on the terms dictated by Allied powers.

Another *Tribune* article on August 14 was entitled "Emperor says Atom Bomb made Nippon give up." Speaking for the first time by radio, the emperor had said to the Japanese people that should Japan continue to fight, "the bomb would lead to the total extinction of the human race". It was estimated that the Hiroshima and Nagasaki bombings killed 410,000 Japanese.

Many argue that the atomic bombing of two Japanese cities saved millions of American and Asian lives.

Members of Headquarters 2 Corps discuss surrender terms with Japanese Naval
Commander Takahashi and Captain E. Kato, Bougainville, September 9, 1945.
Australian War Memorial

Chapter XXV
Surrender and Hope

Buka Island, August 17, 1945

On the day following the end of the war, enemy aircraft, warships and troops on the ground all "vanished as if none of them had ever existed" and with their passing from sight Kawanishi began to realize that, indeed, the fighting was over. The constant tension they had lived with gradually gave way to a feeling of peace and tranquility. A feeling of intense anticipation welled up in Kawanishi at the prospect of returning home and "grew until it became a burning, inextinguishable fire. When will we go back? I desperately wanted to get home as soon as possible."

But there was a problem. A communication from Buin stated that it looked like it might be considerably longer before they went home. Kawanishi speculated as to what "considerable" meant—six months, a year, two years? The news was shocking and tough to bear. Given the uncertainty of a departure time, once more they faced the possibility of starvation and quickly turned to farming. Now that the skies were free from enemy aircraft, fishing became an option. Using homemade bombs to stun the fish, huge quantities were caught, making the food situation manageable.

On September 5, they received a cable from Buin ordering them to surrender. On the same day, an Australian airplane sent instructions for the Japanese to "send a surrender envoy by boat to a point one

Kawanishi, standing with binoculars, and crew prepare for surrender on a barge carrying a white flag, September 14, 1945.
Australian War Memorial

mile down the southern end of the Soraken Peninsula on September 10, at 1100 hours. One envoy. No weapons permitted. The boat will fly a white flag and bring any Australian prisoners and non-Japanese foreigners." Kawanishi described the situation:

> Headquarters immediately held a meeting to discuss who should be our surrender envoy. All the officers gathered were conflicted about the matter. The Australians had suffered a comparatively high level of casualties in our zone and (yet) might be out for vengeance. The wharf engagement, our attacks against their tanks and barracks, our canoe raids—all these things weighed on our minds. No one knew what might happen to someone going alone or what perils awaited them once they arrived. And we found the idea of negotiating surrender repugnant. Officers who during the fighting had been committed to dying courageously in battle now couldn't look each other in the eye. We shifted from one candidate to another: Should the captain himself go? How about second-in-command Honda? The chief paymaster? Or should I go? Those present who weren't being considered relaxed and suddenly became eager to offer opinions on the matter. The four candidates sullenly followed the procedures. Finally, Captain Kato decided that despite the importance of the mission, he wanted me to be the one to go.
>
> I had mentally prepared myself for the possibility of going once I became a candidate, and I quickly got ready. As a representative of the Japanese military, I was determined not to appear dejected and defeated. Instead, I wanted to project the image of a proud and dignified soldier. I got out the formal military dress that I had intended to wear when I met my end in battle, the uniform I had worn when we withdrew from Buin. Though moldy and dirty, it made a splendid impression, especially for one of us. I didn't need an officer's sword; keeping my composure and peace of mind was much more important.

Fortunately, we had no prisoners, and the only non-Japanese nationals on the island were a family of nine Chinese in Nova and four French missionaries in the village of Gagan. During the fighting, we had made every effort to protect these people, and the fact that I had managed island relations worked to my benefit since it meant that I already knew these people. But other than this, I could do nothing more than entrust my fate to heaven.

On September 10, at 0800, they set out aboard two large boats, each flying white flags made from tied together blankets. The 13 non-Japanese were on one boat, while Kawanishi was on the other, along with Warrant Officer Uchida, the boat's captain. Uchida also wore the best military dress and projected a proper military bearing. Captain Kato and the headquarters' officers saw them off.

They crossed Buka Channel toward Buka Bay and the Soraken Peninsula. "The heat over the water," wrote Kawanishi, "was still bearable but the sunlight cast a sharp glare on the water. It was a three-hour journey. The white flags flapped violently in the breeze as the two boats forged ahead."

A wharf came into view as the boats rounded the peninsula to its southern side. A little ahead of schedule, they slowed their pace.

Once we passed the peninsula, we entered Australian territory. We drew close to land and saw a large base built on cleared-out jungle. With the fighting over, soldiers played baseball on the shore. We could also see a building that resembled a cinema.

Neat rows of barracks. Peace. I was overcome with emotion when I realized that this place had been a battlefield during one of our canoe raids. But though this tableau of tranquility lay before my eyes, I couldn't feel it in my heart as I thought about the grave business that lay ahead. I was nervous. I didn't feel like talking to anyone. I couldn't stop thinking about all the things that might happen to us. I kept telling myself that whatever

231

happened, I would uphold myself in my role as an envoy of the Japanese military and never behave in a cowardly or coarse manner.

In battle, a man mentally prepares himself to meet the occasion, and it follows that if circumstances change he must mentally adapt to the new situation. The same outlook will not work in all situations. Besides, human beings are weak by nature, and even as a twenty-five year old man in firm control of his faculties, it was meaningless for me to hold onto the same resolve I had committed to on the eve of war. The boats arrived at the designated place.

From the shore, several small boats with Australian soldiers aboard rowed out to us. Each boat carried two or three men dressed in nothing but swimwear. They shook their fists and shouted at us. They scowled malevolently and spit in anger. Whatever insults they were hurling at us, I ignored. When I didn't react, they rowed back. I remained standing at the bow of the boat with dignified indifference. They had their fun; I maintained my dignity.

Eventually, the appointed time arrived. A big launch came out and pulled up next to our boats. Though it looked like officers were on board, they first had us hand over the non-Japanese. The Chinese couple and their children moved onto our boat. I had met the husband numerous times at Nova. During two years of war, the couple had given birth to two children. I had sent them blankets and covers that we weren't using and made canvas shoes for the children. They were just as sweet as any Japanese kid, and I had taken them to heart.

As the father came up to me, carrying his newborn child in his arms, he said in broken Japanese, "Thank you, captain. This is goodbye. Take care." I picked up the other child, who was now walking and wearing the clothes I had made for him, and carried him over to his father. I said goodbye and saw the man and his family for the last time as they climbed aboard the launch.

Now the French missionaries, their large girths covered in black gowns, came up to me. Extending their massive hands toward me, one said in halting English, "Thank you for everything. We are not likely to meet again. Let us all work hard to rebuild our countries, and may God watch over you." I shook hands with each one as they boarded the launch. The Australians observed this scene from aboard the launch, convincing me more than ever of the wisdom of my island relations policy. The goodwill with which everyone greeted me lifted my spirits.

Now it was my turn. The side of the 30-ton launch was about a meter higher than our boat. I would leave Warrant Officer Uchida behind and be on my own from now on. I climbed up the side. An Australian nearly 180 centimeters tall stood waiting for me with rifle drawn. I felt like I was being treated like some kind of vicious criminal.

I boarded and found myself in a fairly large room with around 10 officers gallantly dressed in military tropical khaki fatigues. These men were probably headquarters and staff officers. An interpreter, who appeared to be Chinese, explained the contents of a surrender document in heavily accented Japanese. Then they presented a single-page light-yellow document for me to sign. I went to a table and signed it. That was all; nothing else happened.

The behavior of the non-Japanese nationals toward me most likely made them aware that we had not mistreated the inhabitants of Buka. The military envoy they saw standing before them must have looked to them like a kid. They were more polite and well-mannered than I expected. My tightly coiled nerves quickly relaxed. But just then the interpreter abruptly said, "We are finished here, but the surrender of Buka is behind schedule and we will immediately go there to take over command." We weren't done after all. I started back for my boat. I wanted to get back onto my own boat as fast as I could.

The interpreter said, "You stay and tell your subordinate what to do from here." I felt like a hostage. Did they think we had laid mines in Buka Channel? Did they really think that Japanese soldiers could be such savages? I ordered Warrant Officer Uchida to pilot the boat and went back into the room on the launch. I gradually regained my composure. I mustered up enough raw courage to see me through.

The room was like a break room for personnel. The officers retired to their own quarters while the sentry who met me when I came aboard stayed with me. I remained in the room, sitting stiffly in a chair. It was now past 1200 and appeared to be mealtime on the launch. A piece of French bread about 30 centimeters long was brought and placed right in front of me. I could smell the fragrant aroma of cooked meat. I hadn't eaten since 0800 and I was hungry. I didn't expect to be fed, yet the aroma of food filled my nostrils.

As scheduled, the Australians arrived the next morning by launch. The Japanese had worked through the night building a temporary office on the shore of Bonis and making lists of personnel, weapons and other things. It was a huge amount of work, but they got it done.

A group led by a young Australian major got off the launch. They were followed by 8th Fleet Communications Officer Commander Takahashi and Chief Paymaster Lieutenant Tsuji. Kawanishi was elated. "Finished with their surrender duties at Buin, the Australians had flown Commander Takahashi and Lieutenant Tsuji to attend to the same matter in the Buka zone."

Commander Takahashi, whom Kawanishi had had the pleasure of working for in Buin, had impeccable credentials having stayed in England as a military attaché and worked as code chief for Combined Fleet. According to Kawanishi, Commander Takahashi possessed a sophistication somewhat rare for a military man. Lieutenant Tsuji, a supply classmate of Kawanishi, was a trusted friend possessing a calm and composed manner. Seeing the two of them filled Kawanishi with confidence.

The negotiations entered the second day.

The Australian major said, "Have all your military personnel assemble at Bonis immediately."

"That's impossible; we lack enough food. Each unit maintains their own fields, and we can't simply have them assemble somewhere. There's not enough food in the Bonis area to mass personnel there."

"Just have them assemble. We'll deal with provisions after that."

"We want a supply of food. The Geneva Convention requires that prisoners be fed."

An argument ensued.

We consulted a copy of the Convention's statutes we had brought. This enraged the young major. He banged his fist on the table saying, "How dare prisoners talk like this!"

"We're just asserting our rights as prisoners."

We weren't going to give in. Indeed, we could not give in.

The day ended with no agreement and the major left. The next day he said tersely, "We will do what you want. Assemble your men after we bring food to Bonis.

"It will take a week to get everyone there. How should we deal with the sick and wounded according to the Red Cross?"

We consulted our copy of the Red Cross Convention. The major said, "Two weeks is too much time to deal with the sick."

"All we need is some way to transport them. We have no vehicles."

"All right, one week."

A compromise. Regardless, Kawanishi felt as though they had achieved victory. Their work done, Commander Takahashi and

Lieutenant Tsuji departed. Again, Kawanishi was on his own.

All Buka personnel were ordered to assemble, turn in their weapons and prepare to depart; several officers who owned magnificent swords threw them into the ocean rather than give them up to the Australians. Food provisions arrived on the fourth day as scheduled and 1,800 troops assembled amidst careful preparation. Seven landing craft arrived to take them to Torokina the next day. Kawanishi details an event that evening;

> *Around five or six islander chiefs stood waiting for us by the shore. They had come a great distance to help us move the sick. When they saw me, they were elated. Behind them, they discreetly held the NCO Navy caps we had given them during the islander relations campaign. They put them on and one said in broken English, "Captain, this is farewell. The captain treated us as friends, and for that, we are grateful. Now we must once again bear the whites treating us like dogs."*
>
> *Overcome with emotion by his words, I said, "I am sure we will meet again someday. Until then, be well."*

The next morning, with 250 men crammed on each craft, they departed the Buka Channel. "I looked back at Buka Island and etched the scene upon my memory," Kawanishi wrote. "The sight moved me to the bottom of my soul."

Japanese POWs from Buin, Kieta, Buka Island and other parts of Bougainville on a landing craft are being landed to begin the march to POW compounds at Torokina, September 1945. *Australian War Memorial*

Japanese Naval Troops sitting down on arrival at a compound south of the
Torokina River, Bougainville, September 30, 1945. *Australian War Memorial*

Chapter XXVI
POW 288045, BUKA

When the seven craft carrying Kawanishi and the other prisoners reached Torokina, the Japanese began a 16-kilometer march to the prison compound. En route three armed Australian soldiers plunged into the column of the prisoners, robbing them of watches, fountain pens and the like. The event, according to Kawanishi, brought home the reality that they were prisoners. Short on water and food, it was an arduous trek that resulted in four deaths and many relapses of malaria.

The prison camp consisted of 20 buildings, each holding 1,000 men. To keep order, 10 officers were assigned to a barrack; at Compound 15, a Lieutenant Commander, was appointed Commanding Officer, who in turn appointed Kawanishi as his second in command. As it happened, the CO was quite lazy, which left Kawanishi as de facto leader. Their first task was to complete the construction of a shell into a barrack that included mess and latrine facilities. The deal: the Australians would provide tools and building materials, and the Japanese the labor. About that time, each compound was ordered to provide work details for the camp at large; Kawanishi sent many more men than asked for, which allowed the extra personnel to wander about creatively pilfering supplies. It resulted in the early completion of their building and won praise from the Australians. "It looked so much better than the others," wrote Kawanishi, which the other compounds found "curious, but we couldn't very well tell them what we had been up to".

A Near Riot

An inadequate supply of food presented a dilemma. Warrant officers, many of whom were longtime veterans, lived with the enlisted men—not a normal arrangement—and began to put pressure on the cooks for extra food from an already scant supply.

The cooks didn't say anything so this went unnoticed at first, but gradually the enlisted men figured out what was going on. The enlisted men, for whom a fair allotment would still have been meager, were enraged. The fact that the warrant officers' leaders included some MPs and a cunning naval warrant officer by the name of Ōshima only confounded the problem. The enlisted men no longer belonged to a unit and it was only natural that their grievances as soldiers and sailors erupted to the surface. Such abuse of power and authority may not be unusual back home, but until then I had never witnessed such deep strife and prejudice in the military.

One night in early October, I was relaxing with some fellow officers in the officers' quarters. After final roll call, we had no particular duties to attend to and everyone did as they liked. At night, the temperature in Torokina cooled, and I was relaxing in a dotera, *a thick, padded kimono— I wore it when I wanted to remind myself of home.*

Suddenly, deck officer Lieutenant Ishitobi burst in, his face white as a sheet. He said that a bunch of enlisted men had decided to take matters into their own hands about something and were threatening some of the warrant officers. Our young unit commander said, "That's the deck officer's problem. Restore order immediately." Now, Ishitobi was a special services officer with a distinguished battle record with the 32nd Construction Battalion. Still, hearing this, he flinched and said, "Out of the question. There are too many of them. I can't take care of it myself." Our commander persisted. "What kind of deck officer are you?" All the officers in the room, however, were beginning to realize that major trouble was brewing. Now our commander said, "Second in command, go and bring them to order." Everything for him was a nuisance. The man was really worthless; every day he did nothing but lie around.

I gave in to the inevitable. After Ishitobi filled me in on the situation, I went out into the prison compound still wearing the kimono. Under the light of a half moon, I could make out the shapes of several soldiers in the lumberyard on one side of the compound. I could hear voices speaking in anger. Quietly, I approached the crowd. After peering for a while from behind the crowd, I could make out what was going on: They were holding a kangaroo court.

First, someone called the names of each of the cooks. Then he called out the names of the warrant officers. With each name, the crowd erupted in jeers and catcalls. The cooks and warrant officers stood before the mob trembling in terror. Cowering in shame, they fitfully tried to hide their faces from the angry crowd. I looked closer and saw that perhaps 10 of the enlisted men's NCOs were standing on a wooden rise leading the proceedings. Despite the moon, it was very dark. Under cover of darkness, they could do whatever they wanted and escape responsibility for their actions. I took a moment to think.

I had no doubt that a riot could break out at any moment. If I didn't intervene and the commotion indeed turned into a riot there was no telling what could happen within the prison camp. I had to act. But I still didn't know these enlisted men very well, and they didn't know me either. On top of that, it was dark and there were a lot of them. The mood turned more and more ugly as they hurled abuse at their former superiors. A chill went down my spine when I thought about where this was heading. Despite my fear, I knew I had to do something.

The experience of years of constant fighting had made me accustomed to making snap decisions, and I made one now. As if to uncoil my own nerves, I shouted at the top of my voice. As a hush fell over the enraged crowd, I made my way to where the accused stood and right in front of the group's ringleaders.

"What the hell are you doing? If the guard tower sees you, they'll turn a searchlight on you and open fire! Have you forgotten we're in a prison camp? What are you doing out here in the middle of the night? Break this up immediately. I heard what this is about from back there. If it's true, it'll be taken care of, but you have to disperse immediately."

Then I was silent. Among the leaders, I could make out the faces of several distinguished NCOs, their faces clearly recognizable under the light of the moon. With an angry glare, I pointed at each of them shouting, "What is the meaning of this?" For a moment, this intimidated and put them off balance.

Then, someone in the back said, "We're gonna get you next." A few others grunted in approval. But after that, not a word. I had won the standoff. "I want to talk to the NCOs now. The rest of you disperse."

Putting still more anger into my voice, I said, "Break it up now!" The soldiers and sailors started to disperse. The 10 leaders, their rage dampened, dutifully came up to me. The others watched this with intense interest. Again, I shouted, "Break it up!" The men began to file off to the barracks.

As I walked with bold, confident strides still dressed in the kimono, I could feel cold sweat on my back. I was so tightly wound with tension that it felt like a different person was inside me; I barely recognized myself.

We entered the officers' quarters. The officers, too, watched with intense curiosity.

"Everyone in here. First, write your name and rank and I want to hear from each of you." I told them to start from the left and take turns speaking. With a look of resolve, an MP sergeant began to speak. He spoke eloquently and

242

held himself well. He said that the warrant officers were stealing extra portions of food. We were completely unaware that this was going on. The warrant officers confessed to this and even signed a letter of apology admitting to it. I burned with rage, as I thought how not long ago the warrant officers, now meek and servile, their heads hung low in shame and regret, had acted so high-handed and tyrannically toward the enlisted men.

After hearing them out, I said, "All right. We'll take immediate measures. I understand your complaints, but what do you have to say about how you went about this? Maybe you think you're no longer in the military, but you still belong, even if only barely, to a military organization. What you did is utterly unforgivable, especially in a POW camp. What would have happened had the men rioted because of what you did? Now, line up over here."

At that moment, I had become someone else. Once the NCOs had lined up, I struck each of them twice with a rod. Some of them even passed out from the blows. I had never before struck a soldier, yet now I meted out punishment with such force that my hands became numb.

Some enlisted men managed to sneak a peek at the scene unfolding in the officers' quarters and quickly reported it to their fellows, sending the barracks into an uproar. "Don't move," I said to the NCOs as I started toward the barracks. Walking with bold, big strides, I shouted, "The warrant officers responsible for this injustice will be punished. But those responsible for inciting tonight's behavior must also be held responsible. If anyone has a problem with this, come out here now!" A hush fell over the barracks. "I repeat: Anybody who objects, come out here now!"

With that, the barracks returned to calm.

I returned to the officers' quarters, where the NCOs were standing at attention. "At ease. I want you to come up with an appropriate punishment for the warrant officers. But remember, for us Japanese to fight over food and

243

the like only brings humiliation upon us. Just what do you think will happen if a crowd gathered in the prison compound erupts into violence?" Then to the other officers in the room I said, "If an officer commits a similar offense over food, he'll get the same punishment." Since I thought there just might be someone among us officers capable of resorting to this kind of coercion, I seized the moment to put my foot down.

The NCOs settled down. When I heard the navy petty officer say the words, "Sir, understood," I was so overjoyed that tears came to my eyes. They returned to their barracks. A riot was averted. The lieutenant commander never showed his face during the entire episode. As the officers in the room left they each gave me silent glances of acknowledgement. My hands were numb. Satei brought me some water. Yet my joy and excitement gave way to unfathomable sadness as a feeling of self-loathing descended upon me over what I had done.

At roll call the next morning, we demoted all warrant officers involved in taking an improper share of food to enlisted men and ordered them to do 10 days of hard labor within the camp. We replaced the cooks. With this, the problem was to put to rest; all abuse of our food supply ceased. We experienced no more outbreaks of trouble over food, and everyone got used to small meals.

With the construction of the barracks complete, life turned into "aimless waiting to return home". To fill the vacuum a warrant officer developed a theater production and put on a musical play using handmade instruments and props. "Each officer dealt with the time in his own way," from lying around doing nothing to studying English, the language of the future.

In October, the Australians closed Torokina and moved the prisoners to islands off the southern edge of Bougainville. They were reconstituted into their original units: in Kawanishi's case, Buka area personnel.

Four days later, he was ordered to join the communications

headquarters on the small island of Tauno. Kawanishi said goodbye to Captain Kato and his Buka friends for the last time (Kato was later executed as a war criminal for his role in the killing of four Buka natives).

September 1945, Stuart, Florida

"The US Navy takes care of its own," the saying goes. The highly regarded and decorated Commander Vernon Jannotta, when back at Navy headquarters in Washington, DC, was assigned as the Commanding Officer of a base at Stuart, Florida, an auxiliary Naval air training station. Perks included a spacious house complete with staff and a 35-foot fishing cruiser. Ordered to shut the base down, Jannotta spent a half day on task and a half day deep sea fishing: he relaxed, drank his fair share of scotch and held forth at dinners at which wife May and his daughters served as hostesses. Surrounded by the people he loved, life was full of pleasure.

By contrast, Kawanishi's life was severe, and hunger remained an ever-dominant force. Also, given that there was very little to do at the communications headquarters, each day was overlaid by boredom. However, Kawanishi found an escape:

One night I decided to go to the sea. I took off my clothes on a reef and got into the water. My first experience being in the ocean was when I came south. While fear of malaria and air raids had made opportunities to swim exceedingly rare, life as a POW brought with it peace, and feelings of nostalgic longing welled up within me.

The mysterious nighttime sea steadily drew me in. The reef-enclosed lagoon must have been thick with salt for the water was very buoyant. I could turn onto my back and float easily. Glittering stars blanketed the sky. I could see part of the Southern Cross constellation above the horizon over the water. As I floated and gazed at the stars in complete solitude surrounded by the pristine silence of the sea and the night-shrouded lagoon, meditations on how

I was still alive at this moment intermingled with a desire to quickly return home. All sorts of things went through my mind. How romantic it would be if a lover were here with me. Where is that young island beauty now, her face tinged in sadness? I gave in completely to the pleasure of drifting upon the waves in solitude...

On February 15, 1946, the first repatriation of men to Japan began. At long last, we were returning home. We would return in three groups. The first group, including 8th Fleet admirals and field officers, would be on the ocean liner and hospital ship Hikawamaru. Enlisted personnel traveled in the second group. The communications staff was last, which was a little disappointing, but if I had made it this far, I could breathe easy now.

On March 1, the long-awaited day arrived. We received only the most rudimentary care on the carrier, but when I ate the meal of barley mixed with rice and miso soup served that first night I couldn't dry my tears. Japan was close. My heart beat faster when I thought that I was truly going home...

Following the coast of Bougainville, the ship headed north. After stopping briefly at Rabaul, the ship resumed its northward trek. The days on the ship were monotonous, but also filled with the anxiousness and anticipation of returning home. During squalls, I went on deck and let the water cleanse my body. Other than that, I ate and slept.

Every day we got closer to Japan. The air grew colder. How long had it been since I felt the cool air of early spring? The mountaintops of the home country came into view. The mountain ranges, still covered in withered and brown winter foliage like a forest become desert, were to our eyes a strange and fantastic sight.

On March 10, 1946, during a rare spring snowfall, we arrived at Otake in Hiroshima Prefecture. My feet stepped upon Japanese soil. I had lived to see home again.

THE END

Vernon Jannotta and Stella Skiff Jannotta at Jannotta's
Navy Cross Board Ceremony.

EPILOGUE

With Jannotta's return to civilian life in 1946, he started a Chicago-based financial consulting practice that served medium-sized retail companies and built it into a successful business that provided him financial independence in the years following his Navy discharge. However, his final career episode came as the result of a Navy connection; his former flotilla supply officer, Hap Chandler, then CEO of Standard Packaging, hired Jannotta as his vice chairman. The size of the company doubled when they acquired the Brown Paper Company of Minneapolis; yet, while the combination provided a substantial sales increase, incremental profitability didn't follow. Ultimately the company was sold for a less-than-hoped-for price.

Now retired in the winter of 1970, Uncle Vernon invited me to accompany him on an inspection of his gravesite at the Arlington National Cemetery in Virginia. Once there, I remember his standing on top of a small grave, a cold wind blowing his wispy gray hair as he looked out over the cemetery with a steady gaze that seemed to say, "So this is where it all ends." Indeed, Jannotta was buried there with full military honors in 1972 at age 76.

Takahiro Fujimoto with oldest daughter, Hiromi,
oldest son, Takahiro, and wife Yoshiko, March 3, 1967,
42nd year of Showa.

In 1946, Kawanishi returned to Toshiba as an industrial relations manager. Through a friend he met Yoshiko Fujimoto and in 1948 they married. Kawanishi was adopted by the Fujimoto family and became known as Takahiro Fujimoto. He left Toshiba and became a successful developer of real estate properties; concurrently he ran the family business, Eastern Motors, a transportation company. Takahiro died in 1967 of cancer, having refused any medical treatment. He is survived by his wife, Yoshiko; a son, University of Tokyo Professor of Economics Takahiro Fujimoto; and a daughter, President of Eastern Motors, Hiromi Fushiya.

Sources and Notes

This book provides a close-up look at the Pacific War through the eyes of Commander A. Vernon Jannotta, United States Naval Reserves, and Lieutenant Kotarō Kawanishi, Supply and Finance Corps of the Imperial Japanese Navy.

In the case of Jannotta, the primary source of information is his unpublished letters to his wife. These began on October 15, 1942 when he described the train trip from Chicago to his first assignment at Amphibious Force, Atlantic Fleet, Naval Headquarters Base at Norfolk, Virginia, and ended on July 21, 1945 with his return from the Philippine Island of Leyte to the US for stateside duty. Since the Navy forbade keeping diaries, letters were his way of documenting his war experiences. This trove of first hand observations in the Pacific was sent to me by Jannotta's grandson (and my cousin) Henry Vernon Nickel, Jr., Stella Skiff Jannotta, Vernon's mother, took the handwritten original letters and had them typed into one document—155 pages, single-spaced. Did she edit them? Knowing her as I did, there may have been editing for grammar and more than likely she removed highly personal passages such as family finances. At the moment, the originals seem to be lost.

All his letters in his first combat tour were subject to censorship. For example, in a November 24, 1943 letter that covers landings on Bougainville Island, Jannotta addressed the censor "(who) I hope, will appreciate the fact that there is no information here that the Jap doesn't already have, or if he doesn't have, would do him any good". On his second tour as a flotilla commander his letters were not censored.

Furthermore, the relationship between my uncle and me was a source of data; in 1950-1951 I lived with him. Many of the stories in the book, such as his getting called on the carpet by Admiral "Bull" Halsey over an illegal scotch stash, were told to me at the dinner table or over a late night scotch. Other stories were found in Jannotta's personal files—for example, the WWI story of the torpedoing of his ship, USS *San Diego*, and WWI letters.

Unlike Vernon Jannotta, Kawanishi made no reference to censorship restrictions, and he did keep a dairy. It was published in

Japan in 1968 as *Bougainville War Diary: A Record of Deadly Combat by a Japanese Imperial Navy Supply and Finance Corps Officer*. He combined on-the-scene diary entries and notes and fashioned them into a book.

Another wellspring is Kawanishi's autobiography. Written after the war and generously made available to me by his son, University of Tokyo Professor Takahiro Fujimoto. It covers his formative years up to age 12, giving a snapshot of Japanese family life, a key to understanding both Japanese culture and Kawanishi himself.

In order to use these sources, I had them translated into English by University of Chicago Japanese linguist, Glenn Rich.

In sum, these first-hand documents form the basic architecture and content for the book. However, to contextualize the writings, the author has interwoven historical narrations drawn from a number of sources to ensure an overview of the war, with apologies and thanks to true history academics.

ACKNOWLEDGMENTS

It's over ten years since I received Vernon Jannotta's WWII letters to his wife from his grandson, "Nick" Nickle. These writings and stories constituted a treasure trove of US Navy WWII history and make up a significant portion of this book. Thank you "Nick!"

Yet, as important, perhaps more so are the diary entries of Lieutenant Kotarō Kawanishi of the Imperial Japanese Navy, who after the war was adopted by his wife's family and took their name, Fujimoto. Together with Jannotta's letters, they make up this book. I feel enormous gratitude to the Fujimoto family who gave me permission to use Yoshiko Fujimoto's husband's writings—and in addition, thanks go to his son, Takahiro Fujimoto, Professor of Economics at the University of Tokyo who generously offered me a copy of his father's autobiography from age twelve, written until his death. It furnishes cultural predictors of the "man" and of his leadership capabilities.

A mid-wife? Yes, this book has one. Roberta Rubin, former owner of the nationally ranked, Book Stahl of Winnetka, Illinois; Roberta has been enormously helpful to me from beginning to end as an encourager, advisor and great friend.

This book is the author's first; John Lofy of the University of Michigan and Sepp Jannotta (my son) of Montana State University, both talented writers in their own right, advised, and aided the author in finding his own "voice".

Extraordinary Leaders contains a number of "themes". Agent Patrick LoBrutto was very constructive in helping organize them into a whole.

The book's designer, Karen Sketch, did great design work and was supportive right to the end. Many thanks go to you.

With appreciation to Glenn Rich for his thoughtful Japanese to English translations.

And also thanks to my line editor, Sabrina Papa, for her good work.

A number of friends have given freely of counsel and editing: my wife Gina, Abbie Fosburgh, Ambassador Ian and Francesca Kelly (cousins), Bill MacKinnon, Pete Henderson, Professor Luke Roberts,

Sam Fordyce, Arthur W. Schultz, Rev. Dr. John M. Buchanan, Karen Alexander, Ned Jannotta (brother), Mary Ireland (daughter), Martha and Jay Mittelstead (daughter and son-in-law), Becky Snyder, Stephen Goheen, Bill McGrane, and Marcy Posner.

Others read all or part of the manuscript: Bill and Mary Ford, Red Delaney, Ann Moore, John and Mary Lohre, Bill and Marcia Littlejohn, Stella J. Kelly (sister), Charlie Jensch, Christine Jensch, Jack Ireland (grandson), Vice Admiral Toshio Muranaka, Rudy Vedovell, Bud and Shirley Bray, Rear Admiral David Polatty, Grace Rachow, and a final note of special thanks to Don Rumsfeld for his eagle-eye in editing the book for correct Navy terminology—and for his enthusiastic support of the book, *Extraordinary Leaders*.

GLOSSARY

AD-2	Single-seat attack aircraft, known as A-2 Skyraider, built by Douglas Aircraft for all three services
APA	Attack transport ship, USN ship classification
B-25	Twin-engine, medium bomber, known as B-25 Mitchell, build by North American Aircraft for United States Army Air Force
B-29	Four-engine, heavy bomber, known as B-29 Superfortress, built by Boeing Aircraft
CEO	chief executive officer
CO	commanding officer
CQM	chief quartermaster
CDR	commander, USN
CV	aircraft carrier, USN ship classification
DD	destroyer, USN ship classification
F4U	Carrier based fighter aircraft, known as F4U Corsair, built by Chance Vought for USN and Marine Corps
F6F	Carrier based fighter aircraft, known as F6F Hellcat, built by Grumman Aircraft for USN and Marine Corps
GHQ	general headquarters
IJN	Imperial Japanese Navy
LCDR	lieutenant commander, USN
LCI	landing craft Infantry, USN ship classification
LCI L	landing craft infantry (large), USN ship classification
LCOL	lieutenant colonel
LST	landing ship tank, USN

LTJG	lieutenant junior grade, USN
NCO	non-commissioned officer
OTC	officer in tactical command
P-38 Lightning	Twin engine fighter, built by Lockheed Aircraft for United States Army Air Force
POW	prisoner of war
PT	patrol torpedo boat, USN ship classification
SBD	Scout Bomber Douglas, naval designation for US Navy Dauntless dive bomber, built by Douglas Aircraft for USN
TNT	explosive compound, chemically expressed as trinitrotoluene
USN	United States Navy
USNR	United States Naval Reserve
USS	United States Ship
V-J Day	Victory Japan Day
VMF	Marine fighter
WWI	World War I

BIBLIOGRAPHY

Barbey, Daniel E. *MacArthur's Amphibious Navy: Seventh Amphibious Force Operations, 1943-1945*. Annapolis, MD: United States Naval Institute Press, 1969.

Baxter 3rd, James Phinney. *Scientists Against Time*. Boston: Little, Brown and Co., 1946.

Benedict, Ruth. *The Chrysanthemum and the Sword: Patterns of Japanese Culture*, Boston: Houghton Mifflin Co., 1946.

Berky, Andrew S. and James P. Shenton, eds. *The Historians' History of the United States, Volume II*. New York: G. P. Putnam's and Sons, 1966.

Brokaw, Tom. *The Greatest Generation*. New York: Random House, 1998.

Brokaw, Tom.. *The Greatest Generation Speaks*. New York: Random House, 1999.

Buell, Thomas B. *Master of Sea Power. A Biography of Fleet Admiral Ernest J. King*. Boston: Little, Brown and Company, 1980.

Burns, James MacGregor. *Leadership*. New York: Harper & Row, 1978

Burns, James MacGregor. *Transforming Leadership*. New York: Atlantic Monthly Press, 2003.

Catton, Bruce. *This Hallowed Ground: The Story of the Union Side of the Civil War*. Garden City, NY: Doubleday & Co., 1956.

Clausewitz, Carl von. *On War*. Princeton, NJ: Princeton University Press, 1976.

Cook, Haruko Taya, and Theodore F. Cook. *Japan at War: An Oral History*. New York: The New Press, 1992.

Cutler, Thomas J. *The Battle of Leyte Gulf: 23-26 October 1944*. New York: Harper Collins, 1994.

Donovan, Robert J. *PT 109: John F. Kennedy in World War II*. New York: McGraw-Hill, 1961.

Dower, John W. *Embracing Defeat: Japan in the Wake of World War II*. New York: W.W. Norton & Co., 1999.

Dower, John W. *War Without Mercy: Race and Power in the Pacific War*. New York: Pantheon Books, 1986.

Dyer, George C. *The Amphibians Came to Conquer: The Story of Admiral Richmond Kelly Turner, Volume 1*. Washington D.C.: United States Department of the Navy, 1972.

Evans, David C. and Mark R. Peattie. *Kaigun: Strategies, Tactics, and Technology in the Imperial Japanese Navy, 1887–1941*. Annapolis, MD: United States Naval Institute Press, 1997.

Feifer, George. Tennozan: *The Battle of Okinawa and the Atomic Bomb*. New York: Ticknor & Fields, 1992.

Fraser, David. *Knight's Cross: A Life of Field Marshall Erwin Rommel*. New York: Harper Collins, 1993.

Friedman, Norman. *US Amphibious Ships and Craft: An Illustrated Design History*. Annapolis, MD: United States Naval Institute Press, 2002.

Fuchida, Mitsuo and Okumiya Masatake. *Midway: The Battle That Doomed Japan, The Japanese Navy's Story*. Annapolis, MD: United States Naval Institute Press, 2001.

Fujimoto Takehiro. *Būgenbiru senki: Ichi kaigun shukei shikan shitō no kiroku*. Tokyo: Shirokane Shobō, 1974.

Gibney, Frank. Sensō: *The Japanese Remember the Pacific War; Letters to the Editor of Asahi Shimbun*. Armonk, NY and London: M. E. Sharpe, 1995.

Goodwin, Doris Kearns. *No Ordinary Time: Franklin and Eleanor Roosevelt; the Home Front in World War II*. New York: Simon & Schuster, 1994.

Groom, Winston. *1942: The Year That Tried Men's Souls*. New York: Atlantic Monthly Press, 2005.

Hastings, Max. *Retribution: The Battle for Japan, 1944-45*. New York: Alfred A. Knopf, 2007.

Hilenbrand, Laura. *Unbroken*. New York: Random House, 2010.

Howarth, Stephen. *The Fighting Ships of the Rising Sun: The Drama of the Imperial Japanese Navy, 1895-1945*. New York: Atheneum, 1983.

Isely, Jeter A., and Philip A. Crowl. *The US Marines and Amphibious War: Its Theory and Its Practice in the Pacific*. Princeton, NJ: Princeton University Press, 1951.

Israel, Congressman Steve. *Charge, History's Greatest Military Speeches*. Annapolis, Naval Institute, 2010.

Jones, Andrew. *The Corsair Years*. Paducah, KY: Turner Publishing Co., 1995.

Kawanishi, Kataro. *Autobiography to age 12*. 1967.

Keegan, John. *A History of Warfare*. New York: Vintage Books, 1994.

Leckie, Robert. *Strong Men Armed: The United States Marines against Japan*. New York: Random House, 1962.

Longfellow, Henry W. *A Psalm of Life*. New York: E.P. Dutton & Co., 1891.

Lorelli, John A. *To Foreign Shores: US Amphibious Operations in World War II*. Annapolis, MD: United States Naval Institute Press, 1995.

McClain, James L. *Japan, A Modern History*. New York: W.W. Norton & Co., 2002.

McMurria, James Austin. *Fight for Survival!: An American Bomber Pilot's 1,000 Days as a POW of the Japanese*. New York: Honoribus Press, 2005.

Manchester, William. *Goodbye Darkness: A Memoir of the Pacific War*. Boston: Little, Brown and Co., 1980.

Miller, William Ian. *The Mystery of Courage*. Cambridge, MA: Harvard University Press, 2000.

Morison, Samuel Eliot. *History of United States Naval Operations in World War II. 15 vols*. Boston: Little, Brown and Co., 1947-1962.

Morris, Edmund. *The Rise of Theodore Roosevelt*. New York: Random House, 2001.

Morris, Edmund. Theodore Rex. New York: Random House, 2001.

Morris, Ivan. *The Nobility of Failure*. New York: Holt, Rinehart and Winston, 1975.

Mosley, Leonard. *Marshall: Hero of Our Times*. New York: Hearst Books, 1982.

Ninth Annual Report of the Board of Education. Oak Park, IL: Board of Education, 1903.

Ohnuki-Tierney, Emiko. Kamikaze, *Cherry Blossoms, and Nationalisms: The Militarization of Aesthetics in Japanese History*. Chicago: The University of Chicago Press, 2002.

Ozaki, Yukio. *The Autobiography of Ozaki Yukio: The Struggle for Constitutional Government in Japan*. Translated by Fujiko Hara. Princeton, NJ: Princeton University Press, 2001.

Parshall, Jonathan B. and Anthony P. Tully. *Shattered Sword: The Untold Story of the Battle of Midway*. Washington D.C.: Potomac Books, 2005.

Peattie, Mark R. *Sunburst: The Rise of Japanese Naval Air Power, 1909-1941*. Annapolis, MD: United States Naval Institute Press, 2001.

Perrin, Jack L. *On A Roll: The Story of Entrepreneur Jack Perrin and Towlsaver, Inc*. Edited by Sally Franz. Xlibris Corp., 2006.

Potter, E. B. *Bull Halsey*. Annapolis, MD: United States Naval Institute Press, 1985.

Potter, E. B. Nimitz. Annapolis, MD: United States Naval Institute Press, 1976.

Prange, Gordon W., Donald M. Goldstein and Katherine V. Dillon. *Miracle at Midway*. New York: Penguin Books, 1983.

Shenk, David, *The Genius in All of Us*. New York: Doubleday, 2010.

Sullivan, Mark. *Our Times, 1900-1925. 6 vols*. New York: Scribner, 1926-1935.

Tillman, Barrett. *Corsair: The F4U in World War II and Korea*. Annapolis, MD: United States Naval Institute Press, 1979.

Tocqueville, Alexis de, Henry Reeve, and Francis Bowen. *Democracy in America. Vol I.* Cambridge MA: Sever and Francis, 1863.

Tregaskis, Richard. *Guadalcanal Diary.* Garden City, NY: Blue Ribbon Books, 1943.

Tsuji, Masanobu. *Japan's Greatest Victory, Britain's Greatest Defeat.* New York: Sarpedon, 1997.

Yoshida, Mitsuru. *Requiem for Battleship Yamato.* Translated by Richard H. Minear. Annapolis, MD: United States Naval Institute Press, 1999.

Wheeler, Gerald E. *Kinkaid of the Seventh Fleet: A Biography of Admiral Thomas C. Kinkaid, US Navy.* Annapolis, MD: United States Naval Institute Press, 1995.

Zweig, Stefan. *The World of Yesterday: An Autobiography.* Lincoln, NE and London: University of Nebraska Press, 1964.

JOSEPH E. JANNOTTA, JR. graduated from Williams College with a BA in History in 1950 and earned his MBA from the University of Chicago in 1967.

Following service as a lieutenant in the US Navy from 1951-1955, which included a tour in Korea as a carrier pilot, he resumed a career with Jewel Companies where he spent 25 years rising to the vice presidential level as a senior human resource officer. In 1976, he assumed the role of president of Yoplait Midwest, a start-up company, and remained there until its sale to General Mills two years later.

In 1978, he formed Jannotta, Bray & Associates, Inc., a career consulting firm with 13 offices nationwide, and served as chairman until the company's sale in 1994.

From 2006-2007, Jannotta served on a seven-member Defense Advisory Committee on Military Compensation for the Secretary of Defense.

He currently lives in Santa Barbara, California with his wife, Gina.

CPSIA information can be obtained at www.ICGtesting.com
Printed in the USA
LVOW07*1919131115

462477LV00005B/30/P

9 781504 950084